"Why have we made elitist that which was meant to be common? Why have we made rare that which was for all? Why have we made Christianity a moral matter instead of a mystical one? The outpouring at Pentecost was the democratization of all religion, and here we have a book of spiritual gems, living experience, and traditional wisdom that again offers God's great outpouring!"

—Richard Rohr, OFM,
Center for Action and Contemplation,
Albuquerque, New Mexico

"Eddie Ensley has done it again. Like his classic *Sounds of Wonder,* in *Everyday Mysticism* he has opened the door for all Christians to understand the best of mystical experiences in Church history. Furthermore, he shows that these great experiences with God are not only for the great and famous saints of the Church, but indeed for 'everyday' Christians. A wonderful book indeed!"

Vinson Synan, Dean Emeritus,
Regent University School of Divinity

"Once again Deacon Eddie Ensley brings a wealth of studied knowledge and personal experience to the topic of mysticism in a way that is highly approachable to the average reader."

John Michael Talbot,
Founder and Spiritual Father,
The Brothers and Sisters of Charity
at Little Portion Hermitage

"As unassuming as its title, *Everyday Mysticism* is also as powerful as the subject it addresses. With simplicity and story and authorial humility, Deacon Ensley opens up to his readers the glory...'the shimmer'...that is the God-experience within time and ordinary place."

Phyllis Tickle,
compiler, *The Divine Hours*

"*Everyday Mysticism* wonderfully shows Eddie Ensley's special gift of bringing to life the rich spiritual treasures from past generations. He marvelously distills timeless wisdom from the experiences of many lovers of God. The prayerful meditations and practical spiritual helps this book provides are invaluable resources."   Dominic Berardino, President, SCRC (Southern California Renewal Communities)

Everyday Mysticism

Meeting God Face to Face

DEACON EDDIE ENSLEY

EVERYDAY
MYSTICISM

Meeting God face to face

TWENTY
THIRD 23rd
PUBLICATIONS
NEW LONDON, CT 06320
WWW.23RDPUBLICATIONS.COM

The stories from this book that involve people other than the author usually make use of composites created by the author from his experience in ministry. Names and details of the stories have been changed. Any similarity between names and stories of individuals in this book to individuals known to readers is purely coincidental.

TWENTY-THIRD PUBLICATIONS
A Division of Bayard
One Montauk Avenue, Suite 200
New London, CT 06320
(860)437-3012 or (800)321-0411
www.23rdpublications.com

Library of Congress Cataloging-in-Publication Data

Ensley, Eddie.
    Everyday mysticism : meeting God face to face / Eddie Ensley.
       pages cm
    Includes bibliographical references.
    ISBN 978-1-58595-843-6
    1. Mysticism. 2. Spiritual life—Christianity. I. Title.
    BV5082.3.E47 2011
    248.2'2—dc23
                              2011047439

ISBN 978-1-58595-843-6
Printed in the U.S.A.

DEDICATION

This book is dedicated to five friends who helped me believe in myself despite my disability

Tom Lawry

Paul Evans

Bill Wise

Mary Timko

Phyllis Tickle

CONTENTS

CHAPTER 1   How Mysticism Can Change Us. 1

CHAPTER 2   What Is Mysticism?. 8

CHAPTER 3   Scripture
The Fountainhead of Mysticism 17

CHAPTER 4   What about Mystical Experiences? 26

CHAPTER 5   Experiencing God Together 39

CHAPTER 6   Miracles, Wonder, Mystery 51

CHAPTER 7   Inner Cleansing. 64

CHAPTER 8   How God Can Change Us
Over a Lifetime 73

CHAPTER 9   Imaginative Meditation
A Doorway into the Heart of God 82

CHAPTER 10 The Mystical Gift of Tears 91

CHAPTER 11 Becoming Channels of God's Healing . . . 99

APPENDIX   Buried Treasure
Mysticism within the Protestant Tradition 112

BIBLIOGRAPHY. 127

CHAPTER 1

How Mysticism Can Change Us

Our hearts are restless, and only one reality in the universe can still that restlessness: the love that is God. Each of us hungers for a love that can finally unruffle us, nurture us, bind up our wounds, and so touch us that we look out at our everyday world with wonder.

Other people, no matter how much they love us, are unable to love us like that, for no love compares to the love of God, a love that is pure, constant, and satisfying. When the need for that love remains unmet, we cling tight to others, hoping in vain they will meet that need. We hold on to the world by the grass. We look to achievements or status, or we feed our hungers with addictions.

What the light of the sun is to a flashlight beam and what the ocean is to a pool left by the tides, such is the love of God compared with all other love.

We have not earned this love; God gives it freely. Neither distant nor abstract, this love comes near to us in the person of Jesus. Those who bask in that love can be called "mystics," and the art of disposing ourselves to that love can be called "mysticism."

As we will see in future chapters, Christian mysticism, rooted in Scripture and centered on Christ, once flourished like spring grass after a rainstorm. In past eras, mysticism permeated society from top to bottom.

These mystics, these "lovers of God" who have gone before us, have left us a vast and nearly indescribable heritage of practical knowledge in how to open up to God's love. Even more, they have left us their own transforming stories. Just hearing these stories opens up bright realities in our hearts. Taking the journey into the heart of mysticism is, in part, a great treasure hunt for something essential that may be, to some extent, missing in our lives and in the life of the Church.

I wrote this book to be more than ideas. I wrote this book to be a pilgrimage, a journey into the very heart of God, a journey that can forever transfigure our world and us.

The mystical journey changes how the world seems to us. As God floods our hearts, we see the world with new eyes, ashimmer with his presence. The embrace of a loved one, a sunset, spring water flowing over rocks, the wonder in a toddler's eyes surprise us, and reality takes on a new splendor.

Brother Lawrence, writing in the seventeenth century during a time of his awakening to God's love, exclaims:

> Natural objects were glorified. My spiritual vision was so clarified that I saw beauty in every material object in the universe. The woods were vocal with heavenly music....Oh, how I was changed! Everything became new. My horses and hogs and everybody became changed....When I went in the morning into the fields to work, the glory of God appeared in all his visible creation. I well remember we reaped oats, and how every straw and head of the oats seemed, as it were,

arrayed in a kind of rainbow glory, or to glow, if I may so express it, in the glory of God.[1]

Mysticism offers possibilities to enrich our relationships, to love from the core of ourselves and to develop what Aelred of Rievaulx, a twelfth-century English abbot, describes as "spiritual friendship." The great poet Dante concurs when he says that "when a soul ceases to say mine, and says ours, it makes the transition from the narrow, constricted, individual life to the truly free."[2]

History is full of stories of people who went on journeys into God's love and whose lives became guiding beacons to others. For instance, crowds in the third century followed Saint Anthony of the Desert, and people calmed down just by standing close to him. Mechtilde of Hackeborn, a thirteenth-century nun, was well-known for her mysticism. She became a solace and a refuge to the sisters in her convent as well as to ordinary people in her community. Just being in her presence had a healing effect on many souls. People revealed themselves to her because she was a reader of hearts who helped people open the hidden secrets of their life in an atmosphere of caring.

Mystics show us that time spent in God's nurturing love enables us to become nurturers. Time spent in the depths of his healing enables us to become channels of his healing. When, with God's help, we face down the terrors of the pains within, an ease, a peace, and a depth of love so permeate our whole personality that we become peace-bearers to all we meet.

 DOUG'S STORY

Part of the mystical journey means facing the wounds in our souls and then meeting the one who can truly mend them—

---

1. As quoted in Evelyn Underhill, *Mysticism* (Stilwell, KS: Digireads.com Book, 2005 edition), 132.

2. Quoted in Evelyn Underhill, *The Spiritual Life* (Harrisburg, PA: Morehouse Publishing, 1937), 25.

Jesus. The story of a man who attended a parish retreat I presented shows how the salve of God's mystical love can transform the deepest hurts.

Doug had been in love once, beautifully, exquisitely in love. The woman's name was Rose and he met her his first year of medical school. Their love blossomed and they married immediately upon his graduation. Over the next seven years, they had two girls, and despite the rigors of internship and residency, their family life seemed idyllic.

Then one morning a police car stopped in front of Doug's house. From the moment he saw the car pull up, he knew bad news was coming. He just didn't know how bad.

The officer went straight to the point. "Your wife and two-year-old were in a head-on car collision and both died. Your six-year-old is critical and just clinging to life at the hospital."

Doug rushed to the hospital to find that his six-year-old girl had died moments before he arrived. He ran into the bathroom, where he threw up violently. Everything around him appeared unreal. The walls, the floor, the windows wavered unsteadily. He entered into a trance of grief. Despite the power of the emotions, he did not cry. His father taught him that boys don't cry.

Doug passed through two years of emptiness and great despair. Everything remained unreal. And as much as he wanted them to come, the tears resisted.

Though he had had a satisfying exposure to Church as a youth, he allowed busyness to keep him and Rose from attending Mass during their marriage. One Sunday after the tragedy, his older brother insisted Doug join him and his wife for Mass. The music that day was first-class. Doug let the melody sweep through him, and unexpectedly and without trying, he began to shed tears. *God cares*, he thought, but the pain of loss remained.

He began attending Mass each Sunday, and every time the tears came, emptying him, sweetly consoling him. He attended a retreat on contemplative prayer, a type of prayer that can dispose us to mystical encounter, at the nearby retreat house.

He then became addicted, with a holy addiction, to prayer. He lit a candle each night and spent an hour or two in quiet prayer and Scripture reflection. At first, he took this quiet time because he needed a love beyond himself to help fill the big holes left by his losses. Gradually, his heart began to sink deeper and deeper each night into the living stillness that is prayer. Before long, he became aware that he was experiencing something more than the mending of wounds; he was falling in love again, beautifully, exquisitely in love again. This time he fell in love with God.

As he prayed, an everlasting beauty and loveliness drew him deeper and deeper into God. He truly began to see God as the lover of his soul.

One night as he was praying, with the eyes of his heart he saw the room brighten with a vast light. The light was alive; its beauty stunned him. The light was the light of God. Doug breathed in the light, letting it fill every cell of his body until he was bathed inside and out with light.

He pondered the possibility of leaving his medical practice and becoming a monk, and he even tried spending one month at a nearby monastery but found it unfulfilling. He needed a more active life; he missed practicing medicine and helping people as a doctor.

In the months that followed his mystical experience, he began seeing a woman, June, who had attended the same retreat on contemplative prayer that he had attended. At first he wondered if it might be a betrayal of God and his late wife to fall in love again, but then he realized that God wanted him to share the love that now permeated his heart. Two years later, he and June were married. Because they were both people of prayer, their marriage became a sublime spiritual friendship as well.

Practical Steps

▶ Think back over your life. Have there been times when you have yearned for an infinite love, a love that could perk you up and brighten everything around you?

▶ Think over some of the times you have tasted that love. Perhaps it was your First Communion, the baptism of your child, a time you looked over an eye-catching scene in nature and said to yourself, *This is so beautiful there has to be a God.* That love is waiting for you, waiting for you to say yes, waiting for you to spend time basking in that one love.

▶ In your journal write a short account of a time God touched your heart.

Scripture Reflection

When we encounter God's love, we encounter his future: a great glory to come that will transfigure all creation and us. In our encounter with God, his future breaks in even in the midst of our human struggles. When we feel restless and disconcerted, it can be good to reflect that a day is coming when all can be mended, reconciled and brightened in God's coming glory. Read the following Scripture slowly and carefully, and let the reality of the coming glory flood your very soul:

> I consider that the sufferings of this present time are not worth comparing with the glory about to be revealed to us. For the creation waits with eager longing for the revealing of the children of God; for the creation was subjected to futility, not of its own will but by the will of the one who subjected it, in hope that the creation itself will be set free from its bondage to decay and will obtain the freedom of the glory of the children of God. We know that the whole creation has been groaning in labour pains until now; and not only the creation, but we ourselves, who have the first fruits of the Spirit, groan inwardly while we wait for adoption, the redemption of our bodies. • *ROMANS 8:18–23*

Guided Meditation

Let your heart grow still. Notice your breathing in and your breathing out. Let each breath remind you of the breath of the Spirit. Each time you exhale, breathe out tension and anxiety. Each time you inhale, breathe in God's love.

Let yourself slowly sink into God's great relaxing peacefulness. Rest a moment in the stillness.

Imagine yourself seated on a folding chair. Immediately in front of you, seated in another folding chair, is Jesus. Imagine him in any way that is comfortable for you. See the holy light surrounding him. That light expands now, surrounding you also. That light calms you, caresses you.

You breathe it in until you are saturated inside and out in that loving light. Be still for a moment in the light.

Look at Jesus. What do you see in his eyes? Jesus stretches out his hands palms upward, and you know what he wants you to do; he wants you to place both your palms in his. You can feel the tension, fear, and anxiety leave you just by touching him. You feel warm tenderness pass from his palms to yours. Rest in the peace of that moment.

Jesus gently removes his hands from yours, reaches inside his robe, and pulls out a beautifully gift-wrapped present. He hands you the package and says, "Inside this package is a gift that symbolizes my love for you." You carefully open the present.

What is the gift? How does it remind you of his love?

Quietly return to this present moment, but retain the memory of this gift. From now on you can be reminded of God's love simply by recalling it.

CHAPTER 2

What Is Mysticism?

The word "mysticism" is nearly impossible to define. It's like the word "God" or "love" or "faith"—words that are bigger than any precise definition. So to capture its meaning we must tell stories, share hearts, and write poetry. In the words of Johann Arndt, a Lutheran mystic from the seventeenth century, "All words that I speak are only a shadow, for the precious thing I discover in my soul, I cannot describe."[3] Rufus Jones, an early twentieth-century Quaker theologian, describes mysticism as faith "in its most acute, intense, and living stage."[4]

In doing the research for this book, I was shocked to learn how widespread among different faith expressions mysticism once was. Mysticism isn't just Catholic or Eastern Orthodox. Throughout

---

3. Johann Arndt, *True Christianity* (Mahwah, NJ: Paulist Press, 1979), 11.

4. Rufus Jones, *Studies in Mystical Religion* (London: Macmillan, 1909), xv.

Church history, from apostolic times to our own day, we find an unbroken stream of Christian mysticism. Neither rare nor exceptional, mysticism can be experienced by all Christians, not just an elite few.

Many Protestants have helped to preserve the mystical tradition through their lives and in their words. They have looked to Scripture, the fountainhead of all mysticism, as well as to the writings of Christian mysticism through the centuries. Mysticism fueled the living flame of God's love that characterized some of the great early American revivals that preceded the modern Evangelical tradition. As we shall see later in the book, many early Lutherans, Anglicans, Puritans, and Baptists soaked in a mysticism that was both real and practical.

Mysticism is not only for monastics and professional contemplatives; it's for everyone—the student who rides the subway to community college every day, the mom who has to raise a family alone, a retired couple who journey into the heart of God together. In short, mysticism is for all believers. The Spirit, whom Christ promised to all believers, makes us all mystics to some extent—men and women who walk closely with God. Jones tells us, "(The mystical life) is life in its wholeness as over against a partial life."[5] As Christians from different faith expressions return to their mystical roots, they draw closer to each other.

One Protestant mystic can help us wrap our arms around the idea of Christian mysticism—Alexander Maclaren. Maclaren was a famous Baptist minister and Bible expositor who lived in late nineteenth-century Britain. Having received a classical theological education, he pastored a large Baptist Church in Manchester as well as heading the World Baptist Alliance. The richness of his abiding in God floods all his writings, and the thirty-three volumes of his Bible exposition that nurtured generations of Evangelicals still remain popular today. He fills his 900-page commentary on John with mighty words that express the centrality of Christian mysticism, calling John the "mystic par excellence" of the New Testament.

---

5. Jones, 17.

Maclaren derived his mysticism from Scripture and from classical mystical writers, whom he calls the "old mystics"[6]—Bernard of Clairvaux, Thomas a Kempis, and Brother Lawrence among them. He defines mysticism as "the direct communion which every soul may have with God, which is the essence of wholesome mysticism."[7] He boldly states, "If a Christianity has no mysticism, it has no life," later adding, "Unless your Christianity be in the good, deep sense of the word 'mystical,' it is mechanical, which is worse."[8]

Maclaren tells us that authentic mysticism must be enfleshed in everyday existence, lived out in the small daily duties of life, finding full force in love of God and the love of neighbor. For instance, he says that Saint John "never soars so high as to lose sight of the flat earth below."[9]

Communion with God, drenching every particle of our lives with love, once brightened Christianity. Maclaren believed that rediscovery of Christian mysticism, of the importance of "abiding," can enliven not only ourselves, but also our churches and even the whole world. He asserts,

> "Abide in Me, and I in you." If…Christianity could only get hold of that truth…I believe it would come like a breath of spring over "the winter of our discontent," and would change profoundly and blessedly the whole contexture of modern Christianity.[10]

---

6. Alexander Maclaren, *The Wearied Christ and Other Sermons* (New York: Hodder and Stoughton, 1893), 163.

7. Alexander Maclaren, *Epistles General* (London: A.C. Armstrong, 1910), 321.

8. Alexander Maclaren, *Exposition of the Scriptures—1 John* (Rio, WI: Ages Software, 2001), 55.

9. Alexander Maclaren, *Exposition of the Scriptures—Ephesians* (Rio, WI: Ages Software, 2001), 82.

10. Maclaren, *Ephesians*, p. 83.

❦ JANET'S STORY

While preaching a parish retreat in the Midwest, I was approached by an elderly Protestant woman who had come to the mission with her Catholic husband. Janet's bright eyes shone with a tender, holy love, and her broad, relaxed smile calmed me. Even before she said a word, I felt escorted into the presence of God just by being near her.

I had just finished leading a contemplative-oriented meditation on growing close to Christ, and she told me, "I've prayed that way since I was a little girl; it's what got me through."

Janet was the oldest of five children. Their mother had died in an accident when Janet was nine. Her father pedaled Bibles door to door in neighboring counties, often taking the money, but not delivering the Bibles. A womanizer, he was unfit to care for his five children after his wife was killed. He would leave them alone for days at a time without food. Janet told me of going door to door begging for food, and digging through garbage cans for herself and her four younger siblings. At age nine she had to become the parent of that family.

She recounted visiting an uncle and his family at dinnertime with her siblings at her side, hoping the uncle would invite them to supper. Instead, he told them to leave. Her two aunts also refused to take responsibility for the children.

Eventually, Janet and her siblings ended up in a crowded and dreary orphanage a hundred miles away, a hostile place where the children could be severely beaten for small infractions. She watched as one by one the orphanage adopted out her younger siblings, leaving her by herself. Loneliness tore at her heart. She dreamed of her father rescuing her and uniting her with her other siblings, but he never came.

Rage and hatred flooded her. God and everyone, so it seemed, had deserted her. Her heart held little room for hope.

During her first year in high school, the Baptist church the orphans attended gave each of the ninth graders at the orphanage a New Testament and Psalms. Janet began to read the Psalms and the Gospel of John, sometimes for as much as an hour a day.

The words descended into her heart, soothing and healing the wounded places, becoming medicine for her. Everything she felt so deeply—the rage and sadness, the loneliness and despair—she recognized in the words of the psalmist, and the Psalms gave her words to articulate her hurt. Also in the Psalms Janet found God's comfort and strength, a "steadfast love" that endures forever.

The promise in John of God's nearness opened her soul. One night after reading Christ's last discourses in John, Janet sank into the stillness. She heard these words whispered in the center of her soul, "I love you, and I will always love you, I will never abandon you." From that time on, she felt the touch of Jesus' closeness inside her. Whenever the temptation to rage came along, whenever loneliness enveloped her, she repeated those words to herself. Without knowing then the meaning of the word "mystical," she had begun a mystical journey.

She put her energy into her schoolwork, won a scholarship to the state university, and became first a teacher and then a principal. Along the way, she married a wonderful Catholic husband, in his own way as devout as she. Because of their strong love of God, theirs became an ecumenical marriage that lasted.

On the recommendation of her husband's pastor, she read many of the great mystics such as Teresa of Avila and Bernard of Clairvaux, finding in their writings an explanation for the love that had crept into her heart long ago. As principal of an inner-city high school, Janet not only motivated her students but loved them, inspiring many of them to go on to do huge things in life. When I met her, she was elderly and retired, but that central flame of love still lit her whole personality.

The doctrine of the Incarnation readily distinguishes Christian mysticism from that of other world religions (including the hodge-podge of beliefs often classified as "New Age mysticism"). Mysticism within Christianity is letting our lives individually and communally be invaded by the eternal lover. We don't move upward to God; he moves downward toward us in the person of Jesus. As John tells us, "the Word became flesh and lived among us" (John 1:14).Most Christian mystics through the centuries did more than sit and count their visions and their ecstasies. Rather than seek altered states, they sought altered lives. Generally, they were no-nonsense men and women who accomplished much in this everyday world.

Catherine of Siena tended the sores of plague victims of the fourteenth century while involving herself in the politics of her era. She even admonished the Pope to return to Rome from Avignon. Bernard of Clairvaux administered a large monastery, becoming a strong and kindhearted spiritual father to all the monks, and advised the Pope and politicians of his day. John Wesley, to some extent an inheritor of the mystical tradition, went into the mines and among the disenfranchised poor, and helped to change the culture of his day.

Today our society wants to divide the spiritual life from the everyday life. As Evelyn Underhill, an Anglican expert on mysticism from the early twentieth century, says, "We cannot divide them. One affects the other all the time: for we are creatures of sense and spirit, and must live an amphibious life."[11]

Sometimes, mysticism is referred to as "something more." I once heard a story that speaks of this "something more" that is open to all Christians. An Italian family immigrated to the United States at the beginning of the twentieth century. They boarded the boat with a few meager possessions. They were short of money to buy food on the ship. After two days of eating nothing, the father of the family

---

11. Evelyn Underhill, *The Spiritual Life* (Wilton, CT: Morehouse Barlow, 1937), 32.

gave his twelve-year-old son two small coins and told him to buy what food he could. The boy went to the dining room and returned lugging a huge bundle of pot roast, bread, and pasta.

When his father saw the quantity of food, it terrified him. "The coins I gave you could not have bought this much food. Did you steal it?" "No," the son said. "It came with the ticket. Our meals are included in the price of our tickets."

For us Christians, more comes with the ticket—our incorporation into Christ—than we ever imagined. We all need that more. We need that love that surpasses all understanding. As I said in the previous chapter, it's a gift we have only to unwrap and make our own.

The doorway to intimacy with God opens wide before us. Your name doesn't have to begin with "saint" to taste his glory. We can all walk through that door. As the Baptist mystic Maclaren tells us:

> Christianity leads us all, to the mount of vision, and lets the lowliest pass through the fences, and go up where the blazing glory is seen. Moses veiled the face that shone with the irradiation of Deity. We with unveiled face are to shine among men. He (Moses) had a momentary gleam, a transient brightness; we have a perpetual light.[12]

Practical Steps

This journey into God with God is not a lonely journey. It is not the journey of "the alone into the alone." Mysticism isn't about navel gazing. It often means walking along the road with others as well as with God. It is a journey together with others. Saint Francis had his associates with him on the journey. Saint Ignatius Loyola had wonderful spiritual friends, and his journey also involved others.

---

12. Alexander Maclaren, *Expositions of Holy Scripture: Romans and Corinthians* (Christian Classics Ethereal Library, ccel.org), www.ccel.org/ccel/maclaren/rom_cor.ii.i.html, accessed September 27, 2011.

▶ Think of a time you have shared in a spiritual experience with others. What was that like? Write a short account of that experience in your journal.

Scripture Reflection

The Psalms have inspired mystics throughout the centuries since so many speak tenderly of intimacy with God.

Psalm 139 is a great hymn of loving praise, paying tribute not only to God's omnipresence in the world but also to his most intimate relationship with the psalmist:

> O Lord, you have searched me and known me.
>
> You know when I sit down and when I rise up; you discern my thoughts from far away....
>
> If I take the wings of the morning and settle at the farthest limits of the sea,
>
> even there your hand shall lead me, and your right hand shall hold me fast.

Psalm 63 passionately asks that God make his presence felt:

> O God, you are my God, I seek you, my soul thirsts for you; my flesh faints for you...Because your steadfast love is better than life, my lips will praise you...
>
> My soul is satisfied as with a rich feast, and my mouth praises you with joyful lips.

In Psalm 42 the Psalmist compares his thirst for God to the thirst of the deer for water:

> "...so my soul longs for you, O God."

Psalm 73 asks,

> "Whom have I in heaven but you? And there is nothing on earth that I desire other than you."

Not only do the psalms talk about closeness with God, they are a superb means of drawing near him. Like Janet, we can enter into the prayer of the psalmist by reading the Psalms as our own prayer. The movements of intimacy with God become the rhythms of our daily life. The Psalms that express the rough anguish of the psalmist can express our heartache also, and the times of closeness to God expressed in the Psalms can lead us into that same devotion.

Reading the Psalms as prayer has been one of the chief ways mystics have prayed through the centuries, and that prayer can attune our hearts to the sublimity of God's presence. The Psalms provide scripts that wake us, express our distress, and console us.

Guided Meditation

Take time to grow still. Let the silence reach your heart. Relax. Just have a sense of a warm, soothing light surrounding you, the light of God's own love. The light soothes you, warms you. Rest a while in that love as fear, tension, and anxiety leave you.

Now that you are calm, imagine that you are at the scene of the Last Supper. Jesus has just washed your feet. Like the beloved disciple, you are reclining on his bosom. You hear his heartbeat. A love overwhelms you as you commune in silence with the Savior.

As you rest there, imagine breathing in sync with Jesus. Imagine vividly what you are seeing, smelling, feeling.

Stay in this scene as long as you can. Just let yourself be drenched in love.

Rest awhile now in that love.

CHAPTER 3

Scripture

The Fountainhead of Mysticism

When the CT scan showed a tumor in my right lung and another in the adjoining airway, I panicked. I always thought that news of my impending death would be easy to handle; after all, I was a believer. Death for those in Christ means homecoming and eternity with him.

Though I knew that truth with my head, I still felt a jagged fear of abandonment. I would be leaving all those I loved—my mother, my aunt, my cousins, my friends, my parish. Who would be there for my ninety-year-old mother if I were gone? God seemed distant. I felt like yelling, "Where are you, God, when I need you most?"

I spent several weeks in tumult as the diagnostic tests continued. I clung to this earth with all my might. *Abandon yourself to God*, my intellect told me, but everything else within me resisted fiercely. I bargained with God. I pleaded with him to let this cup pass me by.

After several weeks, a peace settled me. Whatever happened, I was in God's hands.

When the results of the tests came back, the advanced CT suggested the tumor that was too deep in the lung to be biopsied was a fatty deposit rather than carcinoma. Relief poured over me. Halleluiah! My prayers seemed answered.

It turned out, however, that I was rejoicing prematurely. Three years later, following a set of follow-up CTs, my doctor called with ominous news: two of my nodules had grown considerably, and a third had appeared. A PET scan indicated they were likely all cancerous. The earlier tests had probably been wrong.

Cancer or not, the tumors would have to come out.

My doctor sent me to the University of Alabama Medical Hospital in Birmingham for an operation to remove a large part of my right lung. The operation was risky because of underlying health conditions.

The night before surgery, I pulled out my Bible and read several chapters in the last part of the Gospel of John. The words spoke of Jesus' closeness to the Father and Jesus' closeness to us. I read slowly, savoring each word. One short passage I read over and over again was, "Peace I leave with you; my peace I give to you. I do not give to you as the world gives. Do not let your hearts be troubled, and do not let them be afraid" (John 14:27).

The gentle words rolled by, and soon I ceased reading altogether as the serenity stilled me further. It was as if the mystical closeness of God was a warming light, surrounding me and settling me deeper and deeper into a profound resting in the love of God. I stayed in that deep quiet for thirty or forty minutes, my heart tied to God. Whatever happened with the operation the next day, I was in God's hands, and so were all those who loved me and prayed for me.

The next day, just before the anesthesia took effect, those special words of John's Gospel came to me again: "Abide in me as I abide in you" (John 15:4).

The post-operative biopsy showed stage four carcinoid carcinoma of the lung. The prognosis was fairly good, however. Carcinoid is an extremely slow-growing kind of cancer, and the surgeon had gotten rid of all the visible cancer. I have had four healthy years since my operation, without a sign of cancer.

Like me, many people have felt a mystical calming of their souls through reading Scripture. Because Scripture does more than give us concepts or ideas, it can sink into our souls, touching our deep hidden parts if we let it, creating a mystical experience.

Allusions to mysticism can be found not only in John's gospel but throughout the Scriptures. The Scriptures are the true fountainhead of all genuine Christian mysticism, and biblical images have nurtured Christian mystics throughout the centuries. I was five when my father taught me how to pray. He read the story in Genesis 28:10–22 of the angels ascending and descending the ladder from heaven in Jacob's mystical dream. When he showed me the picture of that scene from the family Bible, it resonated inside me. That image has continued to enrich my prayer life from that date until now. Other parts of Scripture have embedded themselves in me in similar ways.

The fact that Scripture can reach us in these deeper levels does not mean it is merely symbolic. It is still inspired, still true on a conceptual level, just capable of touching us in ways we had not thought possible. And it is in these profound ways that mystics of the past have used Scripture.

The Bible is the story of God wooing us with his love. His light and glory weave their threads throughout that holy book.

In addition, the Bible itself is mystical. Hans Urs von Balthasar, the theologian who greatly influenced John Paul II and Benedict XVI, boldly asserts, "The Old Testament as well as the New, describes the continuous sequence of mystical experiences undergone by the patriarchs, prophets, kings, apostles and disciples."[13]

Mystical encounters with God are rarely just a private matter. They come not just for us individually but the good of the commu-

---

13. Hans Urs von Balthasar, *Explorations in Theology, Vol. I: The Word Made Flesh*, trans. A.V. Littledale and Alexander Dru (San Francisco: Ignatius Press, 1989), 25.

nity. God revealed himself to Isaiah to commission him for service. God asked Isaiah in the vision, "Whom shall I send, and who will go for us?" And Isaiah said, "Here am I; send me!" This has been the pattern throughout the history of the Church. The mystic experiences of Saint Francis of Assisi launched his mission of love and charity, inspiring him to "build My Church," just as Christ from the crucifix told him.

As I have mentioned, I often read the Gospel of John. John calls us to new life. In it, I hear Jesus whispering, "Come close, come very close." For John the word "life" means something divinely begotten. It is life "of God," or "from God." It is life "begotten of God" or "born of the Spirit"—eternal life breaking into the stuff of our daily existence.

Jesus, who is "one with the Father," invites us into that same intimacy. "Those who love me will be loved by my Father, and I will love them and reveal myself to them," he says in John 14:21.

Jesus calls us from darkness to light. He offers his light to all who believe in the same light revealed to Moses on Sinai, to Isaiah in the temple. "I am the light of the world," he proclaims. "Whoever follows me will never walk in darkness but will have the light of life" (John 8:12). That light can remake us, for we are not only called to nearness with God in John, but to also share that mystical union with our fellow believers. John 17 speaks of that goal. Jesus prayed: "I ask not only on behalf of these, but also on behalf of those who will believe in me through their word, that they may all be one. As you, Father, are in me and I am in you, may they also be in us, so that the world may believe that you have sent me" (John 17:20–21).

All four Gospels present Jesus as one filled with the Spirit, possessing spiritual gifts such as prophecy and the reading of hearts and healing that many later mystics also shared. More than a fifth of the four Gospels concerns healing of body or mind. Jesus is presented as the "Great Physician." Many of the Christian mystics through the centuries have also been healers, bringing God's balm to wounded souls and wounded bodies.

When John the Baptist baptized Jesus, according to Luke, the Holy Spirit descended on him in the form of a dove, and a heavenly, mystical voice proclaimed, "You are my Son, the Beloved; with you I am well pleased" (Luke 3:22). When Jesus ascended the Mount of Transfiguration with three disciples, he was surrounded like Moses on Sinai with the light of the glory of God, and like Moses on Sinai, he shone with light.

All the Gospels present Jesus with mystical leanings, intimately aware of the one whom he called "Father." The synoptic Gospels (Matthew, Mark, and Luke) portray Jesus as taking time for solitary communion with the Father. Luke says that Christ often "withdrew to lonely places and prayed" (5:16) and tells of one instance when "Jesus went out to a mountainside to pray, and spent the night praying to God" (6:12).

Personal communion with God, taking solitary time for him to love us in our inner selves, is a hallmark of almost all mystics of the Church. Jesus, like those who followed him, took solitary times for this strengthening, healing familiarity with God that empowered him to fulfill his mission.

Just as John the Baptist immersed Jesus with water, John predicted that Jesus would immerse others with fire and the Spirit. That promise was fulfilled on the day of Pentecost. The sound of a mighty wind filled the room in which the disciples gathered. Tongues of flame fell on each of those present as the Holy Spirit filled them.

As one authority on Christian mysticism, Steven Fanning, boldly states, "The Christian Church was founded in a mystical filling with the Holy Spirit, with the Apostles forming a community of mystics."[14]

Once they experienced the inrushing of the Holy Spirit, the Apostles drew crowds just as Jesus drew crowds. They preached, healed the sick, and performed miracles just as Jesus did. The gifts of the Spirit were not just for the Apostles but for all who believed.

---

14. Steven Fanning, *Mystics of the Christian Tradition* (London: Routledge, 2001), 17.

Peter tells the crowds, "For the promise is for you, for your children, and for all who are far away, everyone whom the Lord our God calls to him" (Acts 2:39).

The teaching of the Apostle Paul was also grounded in mysticism, in immediate, personal spiritual experience as well as in the Jewish Scripture and tradition. Paul came to know Jesus not through the stories passed on to him, but through personal encounter and intimate mystical communion.

The road of revelation was a rocky one. Originally, this Pharisee named Saul had zealously victimized early Christians, capturing and imprisoning them. He had held the coats of those who stoned the deacon Stephen. I cannot help but wonder if Stephen's dying vision, in which the heavens opened up, sparked some kind of inner crisis for Paul. One person's experience kindles another.

En route to Damascus, "breathing threats and murder" against the followers of Christ, Saul bumped into the awesome might of the Holy. Shaken to the core, he saw a flash of light and heard the same Jesus that Stephen had seen at his death. "Saul, Saul," the Lord called to him. "Why do you persecute me?" (Acts 9:4).

After he was baptized, Saul changed his name to Paul and began to proclaim the Gospel to Gentiles and Jews alike throughout the world. To help him organize the early Church, Paul received the gifts of the Holy Spirit and laid hands on those who also would receive those same gifts. Of Paul, New Testament scholar Alan Segal simply states, "He is a mystic."

The road to Damascus was not Paul's only dramatic, mystical experience. To the Corinthians he bares his soul, telling both of his glory and his woundedness. He tells of an awesome experience, which we cannot probe but causes us to stand in awe, "I know a person in Christ who fourteen years ago was caught up to the third heaven—whether in the body or out of the body I do not know; God knows" (2 Corinthians 12:2).

That person is Paul himself. As Biblical scholar William Barclay tells us, "We cannot even guess what happened to Paul. We need not form theories about the number of heavens because of the fact that he speaks of the third heaven. He simply means that his spirit rose to an unsurpassable ecstasy in its nearness to God."[15]

Immediately after recounting his ecstasy, Paul describes his thorn in the flesh. Despite striking encounters with God, he faced the same kind of bewildering hardships all us humans face. He continues on saying, "Therefore I am content with weaknesses, insults, hardships, persecutions, and calamities for the sake of Christ; for whenever I am weak, then I am strong" (2 Corinthians 12:10). The shades of weakness that sometimes plague those who have ongoing intimacy with God are marks of our humanity that continue to humble and "anchor" us.

More than in his ecstatic experiences, Paul shows his mysticism by his living in mystic communion with Christ each day. He doubtlessly was speaking out of personal experience when he wrote, "So if anyone is in Christ, there is a new creation: everything old has passed away; see, everything has become new!" (2 Corinthians 5:17). He saw the same glory and light that Moses experienced, without a veil, residing in the lives of believers: "And all of us, with unveiled faces, seeing the glory of the Lord as though reflected in a mirror, are being transformed into the same image from one degree of glory to another; for this comes from the Lord, the Spirit" (2 Corinthians 3:18).

In his different, unique way, Paul speaks of the same mystical union that John addressed when he writes, "I have been crucified with Christ; and it is no longer I who live, but it is Christ who lives in me. And the life I now live in the flesh I live by faith in the Son of God, who loved me and gave himself for me" (Galatians 2:19–20).

Paul's mystical experiences were for the sake of his active ministry, for the sake of the Church lived out in concrete daily reality. That life of communion with Christ was so life giving he could say, "I can do all things through him who strengthens me" (Philippians 4:13).

---

15. William Barclay, *The Letters to the Corinthians* (Louisville: Westminster John Knox Press, 2002), 304.

Practical Steps

Not only can Scripture guide our thoughts, it can also guide our hearts. The Church has long held to an intimate reading of the Scripture as well as a concept-oriented way of reading Scripture. This intimate way of relating to Scripture has been called *lectio divina* or Divine Reading.

▶ To try this method, pick a Scripture passage that seems to speak to you. Read it several times, slowly, out loud if possible. See if you feel led to offer a short prayer or two.

▶ Next meditate on the phrases that touch you. If a certain phrase strikes you, repeat it tenderly several times as a way of letting it nest in your heart. If it touches your heart, rest in silence for a while, basking in God's nearness.

Saint Ignatius Loyola suggested that in addition to praying Scripture, we enter into the scene of stories in the Gospels. The Gospels present Jesus as a man with a vivid imagination who used image and sensory-filled words in his parables and teaching. As we will see in Chapter Six, imagination is the language of the subconscious.

▶ Pick a scene from one of the Gospels. In your mind's eye, enter into it. Smell the smells, set the scene. Use all your senses to experience the location. Put yourself into the scene as it unfolds. Interact with the people in the scene. Imagine Jesus speaking to you and you speaking to him. What do you say? What does he say? Hold an intimate conversation with him.

▶ When you have finished imagining, let your heart relax a few minutes in the stillness, and reflect on what you have experienced.

Scripture Reflection

Read, in the slow, prayerful way we have just described, the following Scripture passage of the feeding of the five thousand. Put yourself in the scene.

When he looked up and saw a large crowd coming towards him, Jesus said to Philip, 'Where are we to buy bread for these people to eat?' He said this to test him, for he himself knew what he was going to do. Philip answered him, 'Six months' wages would not buy enough bread for each of them to get a little.' One of his disciples, Andrew, Simon Peter's brother, said to him, 'There is a boy here who has five barley loaves and two fish. But what are they among so many people?' Jesus said, 'Make the people sit down.' Now there was a great deal of grass in the place; so they sat down, about five thousand in all. Then Jesus took the loaves, and when he had given thanks, he distributed them to those who were seated; so also the fish, as much as they wanted. When they were satisfied, he told his disciples, 'Gather up the fragments left over, so that nothing may be lost.' So they gathered them up, and from the fragments of the five barley loaves, left by those who had eaten, they filled twelve baskets. When the people saw the sign that he had done, they began to say, 'This is indeed the prophet who is to come into the world.'

When Jesus realized that they were about to come and take him by force to make him king, he withdrew again to the mountain by himself.   • *JOHN 6:5–15*

Guided Prayer

Take a moment to grow still. Picture yourself in a meadow at night-time, lying out on the grass. You are completely relaxed.

Become aware of a light shining down on you. At first, it is subdued, but gradually it increases in brilliance. That light is the love of God. Let it surround you. Let it caress you. Breathe it in until every part of you is saturated in that light and love.

Your heart glows, your breathing becomes calm and easy as you breathe in the light.

As you lie there, Jesus kneels beside you and places his hand on your head. It is so good to be so close to Jesus.

Rest in the stillness awhile.

CHAPTER 4

What about Mystical Experiences?

One of the most painful phrases anyone can hear is "You are not wanted here." We all shrink from those words. To someone in a job it's the feared pink slip. To a couple it can mean dissolution of a marriage. To a teenager that phrase from peers can mean rejection and aching isolation. When I was young, I heard those words too often, and at times only mystical touches of God's love gave me hope.

I grew up in the midst of a great and dreadful mystery. I was born in 1946, a footling breech, with the cord wrapped around my neck three times. The doctor told my parents that if my birth had taken a few seconds longer, I would have been born dead. My parents rejoiced at the miracle of my birth and the seeming miracle that, despite my traumatic birth, I had no disabilities. They were right about the miracle of my birth but wrong about not having disabilities. I had received injury to my right cerebral hemisphere, but sadly, this was not diagnosed until I was an adult.

As a toddler, I seemed exceptionally bright, talking early. I learned to read quickly and soon was several years above my peers in reading level. I comprehended, understood, and expressed myself well. However, I was inept at visual-spatial tasks. Dressing and grooming confused me. Through my teens, I needed help from my parents getting ready in morning. My disability impacted my visual memory. I could put an object down and then forget it completely. I was disorganized, messy, lousy at sports and suffered attention deficit. Yet outwardly, I seemed normal. I suffered from what is called a hidden disability.

Today they would classify many of my symptoms as non-verbal learning disabilities, though my disability was more encompassing than a simple learning disability. School was difficult for me and, at times, I had to endure the ridicule of my fellow students and even some teachers.

College was a time when good things began to happen for me. Belhaven University in those days was a four-year Presbyterian liberal arts college that began the training of many young men and women for service in the Presbyterian Church. The school, set on an idyllic green hill in an established neighborhood of Jackson, Mississippi, was a safe haven from the tumult of the sixties.

A deep devotion to God imbued many of the students. In that atmosphere you didn't have to be athletic or cool to be accepted. I was both wanted and liked despite the problems that came with my disability. In a very moving way, even without my disability being diagnosed, my peers helped me through the tasks of getting up and ready in the morning and assisted me with their class notes, which my disability prevented me from taking with any accuracy.

Graduate school in theology in Richmond, then in Austin, was difficult for me because of my disability. The workload was much harder than in college. I could barely type or handle typewriter ribbons, and my papers were messy and difficult for me to organize physically. My first year I had to write research papers totaling nearly 600 pages. I lacked the close-knit friendships that I had had at college that had helped pull me through.

The isolation bore down on me. I felt a big hole in my heart. My last year of seminary, I failed two courses and had to withdraw. I was told to wait a year before completing my studies. In essence, I heard the phrase "You're not wanted here" from the school. I also became Catholic at this time, the end point of a long, slow journey into the Church.

After leaving theology school, I worked as a volunteer for room and board at an ecumenical campus ministry and Christian community at the University of Texas. We were all required to take part in the upkeep of the ministry; daily chores such as mopping floors and washing dishes were just the sort of tasks my disability made confusing.

I did such a poor job at these tasks I feared the board would tell me they could no longer keep me on as a worker. I faced yet again one more failure. Willing and trying and striving did not help. Something was terribly wrong and I had no idea what it was. I despaired of having any kind of future. Many times I felt there was no hope at all. I blamed myself. Who else was there to blame? Nameless fear, even terror, at my predicament overcame me. What could the future offer me but more failure and despair?

During that time at the campus ministry I turned to prayer. I faced a huge barrier to normal functioning that I did not understand. While all my efforts failed, I knew if I couldn't do anything else, I could pray.

I read Thomas Merton on contemplative prayer and read the Eastern Fathers on the Jesus Prayer. I read the lives of great spiritual leaders like John of the Cross and Teresa of Avila. I read how much Saint Francis, Saint Dominic and others prayed and how that prayer transformed their lives. I would often spend two or three hours an evening in quiet prayer; it was the only recourse I had. I opened up my insides to the love of God. I gained little insight into the origin of my predicament, but I did feel God's hand nurture my soul.

In the midst of confusion inside and out, I felt that love assure me that God held me in his hands, that he would guide my pathways. I remember lying on the floor on my back in the third-floor attic of the Well, surrounded by large windows that opened up on the refreshing night air. I quietly prayed the Jesus Prayer, "Lord Jesus Christ, son of the living God, have mercy on me, a sinner."

As I prayed, I experienced a reality that came like a soothing heavenly melody: one that you hear in the bosom of the heart in the inward silences. In that music the marvel of God's presence touched me, permeating me, the room, and the air. When I breathed, I breathed in the melody. When I exhaled, I exhaled the melody. The music flowed from the vastness of God. Its exquisite loveliness resounded within me and without me, stilling me, bringing great calm. A depth of peace, tranquility, and awe filled me, body and soul.

In the silences, I sensed Christ speaking to me without words, in the language of the heart. I interpreted the message of the silences this way: "I uphold you; you are in my caring hands. All will work out. My love for you will prevail. You will be an author and a clergyman; just trust in my heart. But there is a lesson you need to learn. Your own need has kept your focus on yourself. You need to learn the art of reaching out and loving others. There is a melody in your soul that is your own special melody. If you want that melody to burst forth, concentrate on others. You are hurting and confused, but even in your confusion you can reach out to care for others. You know how much you need love and need others to reach out to you. Reach out to others with the love you would wish to receive. Be hurt with their hurts, smile with their smiles. This journey to reach out in compassion is a hard journey. This letting go, this turning from clinging inward to yourself, is a painful road you must walk. The medicine for your ills is to become a healing balm for others."

Images of friends, acquaintances and strangers passed before my eyes. I prayed for all of them and I envisioned them in my heart. I began to understand that however painful my own situation, I had a duty to let God change me, to say a ringing "yes" to his call for transformation.

The music quieted into reverent stillness, an ineffable, wordless stillness vibrating with Christ's presence. I felt God assuring me that I did have a purpose and that my yearning, my calling to be a clergyman and author of books, would be fulfilled. I basked in the glow for an hour.

The next day nothing had changed; I faced the same difficulties. What I knew, however, was that I was grasped by a marvelous mystery that outshone the dreadful mystery of my yet undiagnosed disability, leading me into a wondrous but yet unknown direction. A few days after the experience, the leadership of the campus ministry informed me I was no longer wanted and would have to depart.

The message I received from that mystical experience was fulfilled. I went on to write seven nationally published books, two of them scholarly research books. Moreover, after my diagnosis and after the Americans with Disabilities Act passed, I graduated from Loyola University with a master's degree in pastoral ministry and a 3.95 grade point average. My bishop invited me to become a permanent deacon—a clergyman—fulfilling a calling that began when I was very little.

I also have preached on the love of God to many thousands of people in hundreds of locations. Confused as I was at the time, as I look back on my youth from a distance, I can see God leading me through the wilderness I was in, one step at a time. In contrast to what I heard from the seminary and the campus ministry, the communication that came from God in the intimate stillness was, "I want you."

At significant times in my life I have had moments when I was struck by mystical touches like the one I described. However, this doesn't make me more special than others or even better connected to God. God constructed us all for experiences of wonder, and many of us have had them.

When God's love floods our hearts, it stirs us. Our unconscious responds, our emotions respond, our body responds, our imaginations respond. The touch of God affects us totally. Our responses to God's touch, we call mystical experiences. As Saint Francis de Sales says, "God attracts the human mind by his supreme beauty, his inexhaustible goodness."[16]

Studies of the average population find mystical experiences to be common, not rare. In *Religious Experience Today*, David Hay reports that several large-scale studies show that 43 percent of all Americans and 48 percent of the British population have had them. These experiences are not merely the hysteria of uneducated people. More than half of college graduates have had experiences of the mystical. Most people don't talk about them and largely keep them private, although many have oriented vital aspects of their lives around them, according to Hay.[17]

Wherever I go preaching parish retreats, people sense that I am open to the wondrous, and they tell me of rich encounters they had with God. Recently, in my own parish a down-to-earth, well-balanced woman told me that during a time of stress, she saw the figure of Christ in her room as she rested on the bed with her eyes closed. She then opened her eyes and saw the clear and distinct vision of Christ in her room. She said she felt a great and inexpressible comfort.

Another study suggests Biblical-like mystical experiences are common among ordinary Christians. Rev. Ben Johnson, a Lutheran minister with a doctorate in theology from Harvard, and sociologist Milo Brekke surveyed 2000 Christians in mainline churches in St. Cloud, Minnesota. They found that 30 percent had seen dramatic visions, heard heavenly voices, or had prophetic dreams. Johnson told a joint meeting of the Society of Biblical Literature and the American

---

16. Francis de Sales, *The Love of God: a Treatise* (Westminster, MD: Newman Press, 1962), 283.

17. Robert K.C. Forman, ed., *The Innate Capacity: Mysticism, Psychology, and Philosophy* (New York: Oxford University Press, 1998), 3.

Academy of Religion, "Two centuries after the intellectual world has said that these kinds of things do not happen, they show up among almost a third of the population in a conservative Midwestern city."[18]

The test of mystical experience is the fruit it bears. As Robert Forman in a scholarly study of mystical experiences phrases it, "When a mystical experience is not repressed and is well integrated into ordinary waking consciousness, it tends to result in a felt sense of healing, renewal, and inner peace and an outpouring of love and compassion for the suffering of the world." [19]

Throughout the history of faith, people have undergone mystical experiences. God touched them and God touched others through their experiences. Those experiences can become signs of glory for our searching world. Louis Dupré tells us that mystical experience has a "remarkable ability to integrate life, to achieve unity within the diversity and complexity of opposite tendencies."[20]

Such experiences are part of our humanity. Our very physiology was made to encounter God. Neuro-research reveals that our brains are "hardwired for God." As happened with me, mystical encounters can rearrange our entire universe. Our Christian tradition abounds with stories of people who had mystical experiences that renovated their lives.

According to Thomas Celano's biographies of Saint Francis, Francis "was almost ruinous and forsaken," when he was led to pray before the crucifix at the fallen down church of San Damiano where he experienced a mighty visitation of Christ and "found himself another man than he who had gone in."[21]

18. George W. Cornell, "Spiritual Experiences Defy Scientific Beliefs," *Daily News Los Angeles*, January 10, 1987, Valley Section, 18.

19. Francis Vaughan, "True and False Mystical Experiences: Some Distinguishing Characteristics," *ReVision* 12:1 (1989), 5.

20. Louis Dupré, "The Christian Experience of Mystical Union," *Journal of Religion* 69 (1989), 8.

21. Thomas of Celano, *The Lives of St. Francis of Assisi* (London: Methuen and Company, 1908), 153.

Saint Ignatius Loyola watched the running water of a stream gurgle by and in an instant was shown the nature of God. The beauty of holiness was shown to Catherine of Genoa in a picture. Saint Benedict saw the world as surrounded by God's light.

The response to such insight, to this seeing of the vision of holiness, is to recognize one's own imperfection and need for purification. Isaiah, on seeing the grand vision of God in the temple, cried, "Woe is me! I am lost, for I am a man of unclean lips!" (Isaiah 6:5). Often, as with Isaiah, the encounter with God involves being sent out to serve. "Who will go for us?" God asks. And Isaiah replies, "Here am I, send me."

Francis de Sales makes the same point when he says, "God generally grants some foretaste of heavenly delight to those who enter his service in order to draw them away from earthly pleasures and encourage them in the pursuit of his love."[22]

Even so, the great spiritual leaders of the Church have warned about making these touches the center of our spiritual life. They can point to God, but they cannot replace God. Our ancestors in faith who spread stories of mystical experiences throughout their culture also warned about loving the gift more than the giver, and of the dangers of seeking mystical experiences instead of seeking God himself.

Also, many Christian mystics have warned about seeing mystical experiences as badges of holiness. Some people, like me, have a more imaginative makeup, and their experiences may be more vivid. But we must always remember that vividness does not equal holiness. The experiences and visions can be pathways to holiness manifested in the twin loves of God and neighbor, but only if we make wise use of them.

On the other hand, so much spiritual literature today readily dismisses or ignores such experiences. This is, I believe, a product of the

---

22. Francis de Sales, as quoted in Steven Fanning, *Mystics of the Christian Tradition* (London: Routledge, 2001), 161.

Enlightenment, the Age of Reason, which insisted that everything be reduced to the scientifically observable and dismissed the wondrous as superstition.

Today we can move beyond the constraints of the Enlightenment and reductionist thought. Even scientists now tell us there is no such thing as a neutral observer. We are always in relationship with what we observe, and what we observe is changed by our observation. This makes room for society and the Church to rediscover mystical encounters.

Many in our Christian tradition indeed express caution, but some of those same people also encourage mystical experiences in other parts of their writings. There is a paradox that Christians have held from the beginning that celebrates miracles, tells miracle stories and vision stories, and then warns against over reliance on miracles and visions. In our most recent century, the emphasis has been on the side of caution, whereas earlier generations exulted in wonders, spread the story of wonders and then as an afterthought expressed caution. Both the celebration and telling of wonders are in the tradition, and the caution is justified. Both attitudes, paradoxical as they may seem, come together in a balanced attitude.

In our own day, sadly, more spiritual writers have expressed only the caution, and this has led to an impoverishment in our teaching on spirituality. Great thinkers like Augustine once freely and unself-consciously shared their sacred encounters. Today many of us keep them purely private, hesitant to let them work their great work of grace in our souls.

For instance, not all mystics had extraordinary experiences. Jonathan Edwards, the great eighteenth-century Puritan and mystic, argues calmly and subtly that, although physical manifestations were not in themselves signs of the working of God's Spirit, "neither were they necessarily not a sign." He argued that the phenomena should be judged by their effects on the person exhibiting the behaviors, for if they produced a greater regard for the Scriptures and for religion, a more virtuous life and greater love for God and neighbor, then "they plainly shew (sic) the finger of God, and are sufficient to outweigh a thousand such little objections."[23]

Saint Bernard of Clairvaux, the great contemplative and writer, encourages spiritual experiences, which he calls the "kisses of Christ." He writes, "Today we read the book of experience...if anyone receives the kiss of Christ...he seeks eagerly to have it again and again."[24] And Bernard inspires his listeners and readers toward such experiences by readily describing his own encounters. He movingly writes of his own sacred meetings, saying, "The Word came to me. I tell you that the Word has come even to me...and that he has come more than once. Yet however often he has come, I have never been aware of the moment of his coming. I have known he was there; I have remembered his presence afterward...."[25]

He goes on to say:

> The only sign of the coming of Christ was a sensation of warmth: You ask then how I knew he was present...when the Bridegroom, the Word, came to me he never made any sign that he was coming; there was no sound of his voice, no glimpse of his face, no footfall. There was no movement of his by which I could know his coming; none of my senses showed me that he had flooded the depths of my being. Only by the warmth of my heart, as I said before, did I know that he was there....[26]

Such experiences are ineffable, difficult to articulate. The person telling of these experiences may use imaginative words to describe them, but even the best metaphors fall short of the astonishing reality described.

These experiences can usher us into a compassionate love of all

23. Jonathan Edwards, as quoted in Fanning, *Mystics of the Christian Tradition*, 192.

24. Bernard of Clairvaux, *Selected Works* (New York: Paulist Press, 1987), 221.

25. Ibid., 254–56.

26. Ibid., 219.

who suffer. They render our hearts tender, helping them vibrate in sync with the world's pain. Evelyn Underhill writes, "The occasional dazzling flashes of pure beauty, pure goodness, pure love which show us what God wants and what He is, only throw into more vivid relief the horror of cruelty, greed, oppression, hatred, ugliness; and also the mere muddle and stupidity which frustrate and bring suffering into life."[27]

Practical Steps

► Reading or hearing about the mystical fire in others' hearts can kindle that same flame in our own hearts. Have there been times in your life when you have been moved by listening to others recount how God has touched them, or reading about such touches?

► Reading and listening to such stories has a way of churning inside us and remaking our interior world. We go through a kind of catharsis as we read such stories. Take time to read the early biographies of holy people, like Saint Ignatius Loyola and Saint Francis of Assisi. *The Little Flowers of St. Francis* provides an excellent source to taste the many varied ways God comes to us. Augustine's *Confessions* is another must read.

► Listen to more than the words, listen to the movements of the Spirit that underlie those words. Read Alexander Maclaren's expositions of Scripture for the vivid mystical imagery they provide of God.

► In a notepad or journal write the times God's love has invaded your life, the times his love has warmed you. The very act of writing anchors those moments in your soul, where they can become quiet fires and enrich all your humanity.

► Take time in small groups in your parish for people to tell one another about the times God seemed near. The very acts of telling and hearing about these encounters freshen our souls.

---

27. Underhill, 82.

▶ Tell more stories from the lives of the saints and holy men and women like John Wesley, Saint Clare of Assisi, and Alexander Maclaren in religious education and in sermons. Let the near-forgotten vision of glory that enveloped whole eras invade our era too.

What is important is the experience of God, not the God of experiences. The real test of all our religious experiencing is whether it increases the twin loves of our love of God and of neighbor. Spiritual encounters are not merit badges, but emblems of grace. Be careful not to think that, because of your religious experiences, you have a connection to God others do not have. Remember that these encounters come to us through our humanity, our unconscious, and our own thoughts, which are mixed in with the experience. Our humanity mediates the experience of the holy. None of us has a pure, supernatural hotline to heaven. Such experiences give us symbolism that is not always that easy to interpret. Simply live with the mystery and let it unfold in your life.

Genuine encounters with God leave us with comfort, peace and a sense of God's own presence. They should also be in accord with Scripture and, for Catholics, in accord with the teaching of the Church.

Scripture Reflection

Take time daily for the silences of prayer and the nurture of reading Scripture. Do more than study Scripture; absorb it in your heart. Read the following Scripture slowly, prayerfully. Let it sink in your soul. After you have read the Scripture, vividly place yourself imaginatively in the scene.

> Six days later, Jesus took with him Peter and James and his brother John and led them up a high mountain, by themselves. And he was transfigured before them, and his face shone like the sun, and his clothes became dazzling white. Suddenly there appeared to them Moses and Elijah, talking with him. Then Peter said to Jesus, 'Lord, it is good for us to

be here; if you wish, I will make three dwellings here, one for you, one for Moses, and one for Elijah.' While he was still speaking, suddenly a bright cloud overshadowed them, and from the cloud a voice said, 'This is my Son, the Beloved; with him I am well pleased; listen to him!' When the disciples heard this, they fell to the ground and were overcome by fear. But Jesus came and touched them, saying, 'Get up and do not be afraid.'   • *MATTHEW 17:1-7*

Guided Meditation

Let the stillness of God calm you. Relax in the depths of his love.

Fear, anxiety, and tension leave you as you go deeper and deeper into his love, deeper and deeper into prayer. His love is a relaxing warmth all around you, as you sink into his presence.

Now think of a time the presence of God stirred your heart. It doesn't have to be extraordinary; it can be just one of those everyday graces God bestows so freely on his children. Remember the time vividly. Remember as if you were there once again. Let the memory relax you further as you sink into God's love.

Imagine that Jesus is seated near you facing you. You can see the heavenly light that surrounds him. His garments appear white as snow. He reaches out palms upward. He invites you to place your palms in his. Feel his palms firmly under your palms. Through his palms he is passing on to you a rich dose of his love, filling you with warmth, peace, and wonder.

Rest in the awe of the moment a while.

Being immersed in Christ's love as your palms are joined, think of people you know who are hurting, people who are discordant with one another, people who are suffering. Let the love and depths of peace you now receive from Christ's presence flow out of your heart and surround those who suffer. As your palms rest on Jesus' palms, envision a way you can be an instrument of peace in this fractured world of ours.

CHAPTER 5

Experiencing God Together

When Deacon Herrmann, who gives retreats with me, and I arrived at a parish in the Midwest to conduct a parish retreat, we could tell that something was wrong. The secretary who met us at the office appeared frayed. The pastor greeted us with a downcast face. He said this was probably a good time for a mission since the parish really needed it. The words tumbled out of his mouth, "Last weekend I announced, on consultation with the diocese, that we would close the parish school after sixty years of operation. The reason was simple: not enough students attended to pay the bills."

The announcement, though not unexpected, was met with grief by almost everyone and anger and bitterness by some. Barbed words against the pastor and diocese came by the rectory telephone. Within the parish, some people passed blame around like a hot potato.

I told the pastor that as outsiders we could not address the issue; it was their internal issue. However, we could lead the congregation into the stillness of prayer where they could meet the One who could soothe grief and calm anger.

During the first evening session on Monday, we gave our standard talk on how the love of God both comforts and heals and told stories of God touching people's hearts. We used simple words.

Then there came time for a meditative prayer experience. In the background, we played a slow, soft rendering of Pachelbel's *Canon*. As I began the meditation, I reminded the congregation how much God loves them. "His love surrounds you now," I said. "His tenderness encircles you; you breathe in the warmth of his caring. He is nearer to you than your breath, nearer to you than your heartbeat, more intimate to you than you are to yourself. Rest awhile in the stillness, rest awhile in Him. Tell him about anything that weighs your heart down, and let him comfort you."

After this, I asked the congregation to relax in the quiet a few moments. Then I invited them to imagine that Jesus sat beside them holding their hands. I invited them again to rest several minutes in the stillness without words. The music tapered off into sheer silence.

As I looked over the congregation, the faces showed that the people were profoundly absorbed in prayer. A few people reached for Kleenex as tears began softly trickling down their faces. No one spoke out a word; no one needed to. A heartfelt sense of God's love filled us all, it seemed.

After the time of meditation was over, people commented on how near God seemed. As one woman told me, "It was as though there were a bright cord of light that went through each of us, binding heart to heart. It was as though a caring, loving light engulfed us all together."

In the midst of such a great love, people told me they forgot, for a while, their anger over the school's closing. They formed one people, one family, one flock with hearts in accord; that unity and that love was all that was important. They could now begin the process of healing after the awful news of the school's closing. God still had a mission for them as a parish—even without a school. They were still called, still sent, still his disciples.

Together we experienced a group mystical experience. Each of us had a unique experience of Jesus, but there was a common love that knit us together.

Too often, we tend to think of mystical experience as a highly individualized, even lonely, quest for God. Sadly, too much of the contemporary literature on mysticism gives us that impression.

Actually, mystical experience is contagious, caught more than taught. Quaker mystic Rufus Jones tells how as a child he learned to experience God through the contagion of being near people who felt God. As a child he attended silent prayer sessions in which people disposed themselves to the One Love. He writes, "There was something contagious about the silence. It caught us all into its living fold. The persons who composed the group were, for the most part, simple, rustic people who came from their farms and their kitchens, but one felt that they knew God and found Him there....There was a touch of awe and majesty, of surprise and wonder...there was a gleam of eternal reality breaking on the humble group...."[28]

In the past thirty years of leading retreats, I have witnessed that contagion of God's presence spread over groups of people many times. I have seen times when all of us felt as one the inward stirrings of the Spirit. Silence seeded with stories of our mysterious God can unite us in one timeless moment.

Hearing of the lives and personal encounters of people from the past as well as the present allows us to catch the flame that burned in their hearts. As Rufus Jones goes on to say, "Mystical experience is more or less transmissive and contagious, as all experiences of intensity are likely to be."[29]

---

28. Rufus Jones, *Essential Writings* (Maryknoll, NY: Orbis Books, 2001).

29. Rufus Jones, *Some Exponents of Mystical Religion* (New York, Cincinnati: Abingdon Press, 1930), 22.

Going back to some of the earliest mystics, we find striking examples of group mystical experience. A towering point in the story of mysticism is Saint Augustine and his congregation in Hippo, now located in modern-day Algeria, in the late fourth and early fifth centuries. The great twentieth-century expert on Western mysticism, Cuthbert Baker, called him the "prince of the mystics" because of his blend of sweeping intellectual grasp of the love of God combined with his heartfelt inner experience of that same love.

Born to a pagan father and to Saint Monica, a devoutly Christian mother, Augustine excelled in his studies. Augustine had a mistress for thirteen years and fathered a son, Adeodatus. Later, he underwent a profound conversion to Christianity and went on to become a leading theologian and bishop.

Augustine wrote many books, including *The Confessions*, the story of his life written as an open letter to God. His works had a profound influence on the Christian scholars who followed him. His warm imagination permeates his writing. Augustine's powerful emotive writing shows him to be a mystic: "Too late have I loved you, O Beauty so ancient and so new."[30] Then again, he speaks of the intimate inner presence of God, saying, "And sometimes you cause me to enter into an extraordinary depth of feeling marked by a strange sweetness. If it were brought to perfection in me, it would be an experience quite beyond anything in this life."[31]

We need to remember that Augustine lived an interior life while actively pastoring a church in Hippo. He describes touches of the mystical, not only in the lives of the clergy and monks but also in the lives of ordinary people in his congregation. He recounts many miracles, visions and contacts with God in their midst.

He describes simple Psalm singing by his congregation as accompanied by deep currents of God's love flowing within the

---

30. Agostino Trape, *St. Augustine: Man, Pastor, Mystic* (New York: Catholic Book Publishing Corporation, 1991), 266.

31. Saint Augustine, as quoted in Fanning, 78.

crowd. Many possessed what mystic writers call "the gift of tears." Augustine recounts one young boy's experience of the holy during the Liturgy:

> You will see him singing with intense emotion, with the ex-pression of his face adapting itself to the spirit of the psalm and with tears often coursing down his cheeks. He sighs be-tween the words that he sings, and whoever has no special skill in reading men's thoughts will be wholly taken in by the outward appearance and will say: "How deeply this lad is stirred as he listens to this psalm!" See how he sighs, how deeply he sighs.[32]

Augustine believed that nothing less than miracles happened in the midst of the people who formed his congregation. In the twenty-second chapter of his monumental work *The City of God*, Augustine describes such miracles, many of which he witnessed personally. The miracles sometimes involved visions on the part of ordinary people as well as group mystical experience.

The church in Hippo was also a shrine to Saint Stephen the martyr. The people believed Christ blessed them with healings, in part through the intercession of Stephen. Augustine relates the healing of two young people, a sister and a brother, who appeared to suffer from a neurological disorder that caused shaking and some-times convulsions. In a dream vision, they were told to go to the shrine of Saint Stephen, where they would be healed. According to Augustine, that healing came on Easter. As the Liturgy began, the brother began to convulse. As he touched the railing of the shrine, he was healed instantly. Augustine took the young man in his arms before the whole congregation, tenderly embracing him. Soon af-terward, his sister was healed. The congregation responded in amazement.

Augustine writes, "Such wonder rose up from men and women

---

32. Frederick van der Meer, Brian Battershaw, G.R. Lamb, *Augustine the Bishop: The Life and Work of a Father of the Church* (New York: Sheed and Ward, 1961), 336.

together that the exclamations and tears seemed as if they would never come to an end."[33]

Augustine describes mysticism flowering in the midst of normal living. Moving experiences of God were not just for desert saints or monks, but for lives lived out in a real world. The people of Augustine's church knew how to dispose themselves to the love of God, and not just individually but together.

Mystical experiences pervade all of Christian history. In 1145, a revival of spiritual experience occurred in Normandy. People everywhere, it seemed, turned to God. They made peace with neighbors and repented of sin. As eyewitness Abbot Haimon reported, God drew them into "a new way of seeking him."[34] It is reported that tears coursed down the eyes of the people, and they responded to the beauty that they felt by banding together in associations to begin the construction of Chartres Cathedral. Priests exhorted them to greater conversion of heart. Princes joined together with serfs to do the building.

Haimon's words leap across the centuries:

> For whoever beheld, who ever heard, in all the ages past that kings, princes, the powerful men of this world…used to a life of ease harness themselves to a wagon and haul a load of stone When they stopped nothing was heard but pure prayer to God hatreds ceased, grudges disappeared and men's hearts were united.[35]

---

33. Saint Augustine of Hippo, *City of God*, A select library of the Nicene and post-Nicene fathers of the Christian Church, books.google.com/books?id=tzwwAAAA YAAJ&pg=PA491&lpg=PA491&dq=Such+wonder+rose+up+from+men+and+wo men+together+that+the+exclamations+and+tears+seemed+as+if+they+would+n ever+come+to+an+end&source=bl&ots=oiLnFH-ae6&sig=t3gYKlF6p21v9f3PbiV AVIwLGQs&hl=en&ei=2fqATpn3E4vViAKM_-n0DA&sa=X&oi=book_result&c t=result&resnum=1&ved=0CBwQ6AEwAA#v=onepage&q=Such%20wonder%20 rose%20up%20from%20men%20and%20women%20together%20that%20the%20 exclamations%20and%20tears%20seemed%20as%20if%20they%20would%20 never%20come%20to%20an%20end&f=false. (Accessed September 26, 2011.)

34. G.G. Coulton, *Life in the Middle Ages, Volume III, Men and Manners* (New York: Macmillan, 1930), 18–22.

35. Ibid., 18–22.

A cathedral began its soar to the sky, expressing God's glory. At night people gathered around the beginnings of the high altar. Haimon reports that many physical and emotional healings occurred then, as well as throughout the day's work, saying, "If I would tell all that I have been allowed to see, even in a single night, my memory and my tongue would utterly fail me."[36]

During the moving of the stone used to construct the cathedral, the wagons would stop and the sick were prayed for. Haimon says, "[Y]ou may see the dumb open their mouths to praise God. Those troubled by demons come to sounder mind….The sick and those troubled by various diseases get up healed from the wagons on which they have been laid."[37]

One of the greatest saints was also a great mystic. Saint Francis was one whose contagious love of God tenderly spread to those who met him. People felt God's presence just by being near him. Bonaventure, in his *The Life of St. Francis of Assisi [Fom the Legenda Sancti Francisci]*, tells the delightful story of an abbot who visited Francis to talk about his soul. He asked Francis to pray for him, and as Francis prayed, suddenly the abbot felt in his

> spirit an unusual warmth and sweetness such as he had never before experienced, so much so that he was rapt in ecstasy and totally lost himself in God. He remained so for a short while, and when he came back to himself, recognized the power of St. Francis in prayer. After that he always burned with a greater love for the Order and related the event to many as a miracle.[38]

The original sources on the life of Saint Francis and his early followers give numerous examples of mystical experiences in the midst

---

36. Ibid., 18–22

37. Ibid., 18–22.

38. Saint Bonaventure, *Bonaventure (Classics of Western Spirituality)*, trans. Ewert Cousins (Mahwah, NJ: Paulist Press, 1978), 276–77.

of acts of ministry. In particular, *The Little Flowers of St. Francis* shows how one person's holy encounter could kindle another's, spreading like a contagion, and how all such encounters supported an active ministry of loving service. *The Little Flowers* contains the most cherished memories and traditions of his early companions. At the same time, it may well contain a touch of the legendary. Scholarship does not provide us the tools to judge the accuracy of these traditions in *The Little Flowers*, but we can say that people believed mystical experiences happened frequently and that often two or more people were caught up in or affected by the encounter.

One such encounter is an experience both Francis and his spiritual friend Clare shared. Francis often met with Clare to discuss spiritual matters. One day she shared a meal with Francis in front of the church of St. Mary of the Angels. Francis prepared the meal on the bare ground as he was accustomed to do. Brother Ugolino reports, "When the first dish was served, Francis began to speak of God so sweetly, so sublimely, and in a manner so wonderful, that the grace of God visited them abundantly, and all were rapt in Christ." People nearby saw the church and the place where Clare and Francis were eating surrounded in flames. The rushed to St. Mary's to put out the flames. When they arrived, they found no fire. Instead, they saw Francis and Clare and their companions sitting around absorbed in contemplation. Then they knew certainly "that which they had seen was a celestial fire, not a material one, which God miraculously had sent to bear witness to the divine flame of love which consumed the souls of those holy brethren and nuns." The people returned home, after witnessing this sacred moment, "with great consolation in their hearts…"[39]

The early lives of Francis and his followers contain many similar instances when the love of God was "caught" by people just being near a group or an individual whose heart blazed with God's presence.

Perhaps the most beautiful description of a group united as one by mystical experience ever written is the account by Thomas of

---

39. Brother Ugolino, *The Little Flowers of St. Francis of Assisi* (CCEL, public domain), XV.

Celano of the canonization of Francis in Assisi. The life of Francis had been lived like a lyric poem. His love, his strength, and his tenderness had touched tens of thousands before his death. When the announcement came that the Pope was to declare Francis a saint, people danced in the streets.

He says that when the day arrived, the city was "filled with gladness," the crowd of people marked the occasion "with great jubilation, and the brightness of the day was made brighter by the torches they brought."

Then he gives the account of the actual canonization. (This is a first-hand account; he was doubtless present at the canonization.) An account was read of the life and miracles of Francis. The Pope was so moved by this account that he

> breathed deep sighs that rose from the bottom of his heart, and, seeking relief in repeated sobs, he shed a torrent of tears. The other prelates of the Church likewise poured forth a flood of tears, so that their sacred vestments were dampened by the abundant flow. Then all the people began to weep.

The Pope lifted up his hands to heaven and proclaimed Francis enrolled among the saints.

> At these words the reverend cardinals, together with the Lord Pope, began to sing the *Te Deum* in a loud voice. Then there was raised a clamor among the many people praising God: the earth resounded with their mighty voices, the air was filled with their jubilations, and the ground was moistened with their tears. New songs were sung, and the servants of God jubilated in melody of the Spirit. Sweet sounding organs were heard there and spiritual hymns were sung with well-modulated voices. There a very sweet odor was breathed, and a most joyous melody that stirred the emotions resounded there.[40]

---

40. Thomas of Celano, *St. Francis of Assisi: First and Second Life of St. Francis with Selections from the Treatise on the Miracles of Blessed Francis*, trans. Placid Hermann (Chicago: Franciscan Herald Press, 1963), 69.

It was after the account of Francis' life was read before the group at his canonization that the tender presence of God descended on the crowd.

Practical Steps

People crave the wonder of tasting God together as a family of faith. Parishes can offer contemplative prayer meetings using both guided meditations and silence.

► Perhaps before the actual prayer, mystical stories from Scripture or our 2,000-year-old Christian heritage can be retold, easing people's hearts into a shared group experience and seeding the quiet with wonder.

► Recalling those together inclines our hearts as one and unites us to that same group encounter with God. We taste that which was already present in the depths of our souls.

Also, most of us have people in our lives, a teacher, a pastor, a family member, who seemed saturated in the love of God. Just drawing close to such people often stirs our hearts. I think of the effect John Paul II had on crowds, especially crowds of young people. The love that fired his heart spread to those present. Mother Teresa of Calcutta had that same effect.

► Recounting the experiences of those who have gone before as well as the experiences of people today can fire our souls with the same flame, individually and together.

► In your journal recall a time when you experienced God's presence together with others, and write about it.

Scripture Reflection

Place yourself at the scene of this Scripture, the Ascension. See the cloud, see Jesus lifted up, feel the glory of the moment.

So when they had come together, they asked him, 'Lord, is this the time when you will restore the kingdom to Israel?' He replied, 'It is not for you to know the times or periods that the Father has set by his own authority. But you will receive power when the Holy Spirit has come upon you; and you will be my witnesses in Jerusalem, in all Judea and Samaria, and to the ends of the earth.' When he had said this, as they were watching, he was lifted up, and a cloud took him out of their sight.   • *ACTS 1:6–9*

Guided Meditation

Let yourself grow still. Notice your breathing. Each time you breathe out, breathe out fear, tension and anxiety. Each time you breathe in, breathe in God's presence.

Let God's merciful care surround you, calming you, assuring you, easing you.

Gently repeat over and over again a short prayer, such as the name "Jesus," to further still you.

Imagine that you are standing in a large meadow holding an unlit candle. It's nighttime and there is a clear sky bursting with stars; a half moon lights up the sky. As you breathe in the fresh air, also smell the aroma of the grass and spring blossoms. It's good to be there absorbing the beauty.

Next to you stands Jesus; you can see the light of his peace surrounding him. He tells you to take a moment and turn your senses inward, sensing physical or emotional pain. He tells you to talk to him about that pain.

Empty your heart out before him.

He puts a hand on your head, and peace flows from the top of your head, through your torso, arms and legs and feet, until you are thoroughly infused from head to toe with the peace of Jesus.

You look to your other side and behind you, and you see a crowd of people, the people who have helped, taught and loved you well through your life. Each one holds a lighted candle. The person to your left smiles and lights your candle. Together you see the lighted faces of each person. The light grows larger and brighter than mere candle light. An orb of light now encircles all of you, joining with the holy light that surrounds Jesus. You all lock arms and stand in awe of the majestic presence that is God.

Stand there as long as you wish.

CHAPTER 6

Miracles, Wonder, Mystery

What is a miracle? The idea that miracles always involve the breaking or suspension of a fixed natural law is relatively new. Our ancestors in faith regarded a miracle as anything that inspired awe. Everything was both natural and wondrous at the same time. During the age of the Fathers and Mothers of the Church and the medieval period, literature is full of these sorts of "miracles."

Wherever mysticism has flourished, one often finds healings, miracles and wonders—not just among the saints, but even among ordinary people. We see just how deeply mysticism penetrated the lives of ordinary people in what are sometimes called the "books of miracles." When someone was sick or injured in medieval cities or villages, a crowd of people would gather around praying for that person. If a healing or miracle took place, a pilgrimage was made from the location of the miracle to a shrine to give thanks. At the shrine the witnesses would give sworn firsthand depositions of the whole miracle story. Thousands of sick people would also journey to the shrine seeking healing. When healings occurred, their depositions would often be taken.

These depositions, which are perhaps the best source of information about everyday life among average people, are just now being made available to scholars. Thousands of these accounts were collected and clearly demonstrate that wonders were a part of everyday lives not just in "contrived" saint's stories.

KEVIN'S STORY

Throughout my thirty years of giving parish missions and retreats, I have heard many people recount what can only be called miracles. One miracle involved Kevin, a retired dentist in his mid-sixties who came reluctantly to a parish mission Deacon Herrmann and I led in the Northeast. He came only because a friend pressured him to do so.

His late wife, Nora, had been a devout believer, but he attended Mass with her only sporadically most of their married life. If asked then if he believed in God, he would have said a hesitant yes. Nora, however, was the world to him. They had never had children, but that never mattered; they found rich companionship in each other. Their hearts beat as one. They loved to take long vacations in their recreational vehicle, going wherever they took a notion to go. On one trip, as they drove through a large city, they passed a demolition site where a machine wielding a ball on a chain tore away at an old building. Just as their vehicle passed near the site, the wrecking ball tumbled out of control, hitting Nora's side of the vehicle, killing her instantly.

Kevin's only family was lost in a second. He found himself alone, forsaken and with little to live for. If there were a God, how could he let something so tragic happen? It was almost as though Kevin were consigned to solitary confinement with hardly anyone or anything to warm his heart with companionship. He raged at God and finally came to believe that he would prefer to believe there was no God than to view God as a monster who took away his wife.

The first night he attended the parish mission with his friend, I led the group in guided stillness prayer and guided imagery prayer. I had them imagine that Jesus was seated beside them and taking their hands in his. I asked them to feel the place in his hand where the nail had been. I encouraged them to feel the healing warmth of his love pass from his hand to theirs and fill them body and soul with Jesus' soothing warmth.

I could see Kevin's muscles relax as I spoke of Jesus holding his hand. He was being drawn deeply into the meditation, going deeper and deeper into prayer. Then I heard him make a guttural sound and, just above a whisper, say "no" twice, then open his eyes.

When he recounted his experience to me the next night, he said he had felt Jesus come close to him comforting him, the first comfort he had felt since his wife's death. Then he hit a wall, and he pulled himself back from the nearness of Jesus and opened his eyes. He couldn't let himself believe in what he thought was an illusion; he had to push God away one more time.

That night he dreamed a vivid dream in a way that was "realer than real," as he put it. His wife, breathing and living, surrounded by light, walked into his room. She came up close to him and brushed his forehead with her hand. A sense of awe, comfort, and wonder passed through him. She was really there. Real as his heart that was now beating rapidly in his chest. "I've missed you so much," he said to her. She smiled and said, "I love you and miss you too."

She then looked at the open door to the bedroom and said, "Here is someone I want you to meet."

He looked at the door and then Jesus, surrounded by heavenly light, walked through the door, stood beside the bed and also comforted him with a hand brushed across his forehead. "Don't fear me, Kevin," he said. "I suffered with you in your loneliness and isolation, and I am always here to help you. Come to me often."

Then they disappeared. Kevin said he wasn't sure if it had all been a dream, but if it was, it was a dream more alive than life itself. Whether asleep or awake, he knew Jesus had visited him and that his life would never be the same.

Kevin began attending Mass regularly, coming to the sacraments often, and developing a deep prayer relationship with Jesus. He joined the Knights of Columbus, a fraternal organization for Catholic men, and made several sustaining spiritual friendships. And he told the story often of his "miracle" that set his feet on the pathway into God with God.

Young children see the whole world as miracle. When we go on a purifying journey with God into God, we become more child-like; the world becomes fresh to us, and we see his miracles everywhere. We regain the child-like ability to see the whole of life as miracle, a worldview that permeated both the patristic era and the Middle Ages. As medievalist Benedicta Ward puts it, "miracles formed an integral part of everyday life. [They were] closely woven into the texture of Christian experience."[41] This heritage remains in the expectant crowds of Lourdes and other shrines, such as Santiago de Compostela, which have attracted pilgrims for centuries.

We may not see many of the more stupendous miracles, but if we look with eyes of faith, we can stand in astonishment at the touch of

---

41. Benedicta Ward, *Miracles and the Medieval Mind: Theory, Record, and Event, 1000–1215 (The Middle Ages Series)* (Philadelphia: University of Pennsylvania Press, 1987), 1–2.

God's hand in our daily world: the small "miracles of the heart" that are not really so small after all.

We don't share our experience of wonder as readily today as Christians once did. We have partially lost touch with a wondrous heritage that extends from Pentecost till our own day.

We have accounts of many thousands of wondrous spiritual happenings through the centuries. Yet sadly, they are most always not reflected in the modern histories of the Church or books on mysticism. For too long Church historians have simply ignored the sources that describe miracles and wonder, and this leaves us with an impoverished history.

The Church throughout the ages kept accounts of these touches of the divine, but all too often these accounts, many of them first-hand, are not appropriated or used to help us with our spirituality today. In the past, stories were one of the most important, if not the most important, ways the fires of mysticism spread. Ignatius Loyola read stories on the miracles and lives of the saints that prepared him for the mystical experiences that were part of his conversion. Too many modern guides to spirituality leave out these stories of wonder, presenting only the dry intellectual, theological theories of mysticism and passing over the thousands of stories of the wondrous in people's lives.

Many great figures have accounts of encounters with the wondrous that happened in their own day. Augustine, for instance, left us important records of his own spiritual experiences in his *Confessions*. He describes the touch of the mystical at the time of his conversion:

> Late have I loved you, O Beauty ever ancient, ever new, late have I loved you!…You called, you shouted, and you broke through my deafness. You flashed, you shone, and you dispelled my blindness….I have tasted you, now I hunger and thirst for more.[42]

---

42. Saint Augustine, *Augustine of Hippo, Selected Writings* (New York: Paulist Press, 1984), 144.

Even more importantly, in his great book *The City of God*, Augustine left us an account of the many amazing happenings among ordinary people in the congregation of his church in Hippo, where he pastored as bishop as well as in nearby regions. Many of the stories were a blend of mystical experience and healing. He either witnessed these healings firsthand or received the accounts from witnesses.

In one especially moving report, he tells about a mystical experience and healing that saved the life of a devout Carthaginian woman named Innocentia. Her physicians diagnosed her with incurable cancer of the breast. Surgery wouldn't help in this case, and there was nothing left to do except let the disease run its deadly course.

Innocentia began to pray fervently to God for a healing of the cancer. Near Easter, she had a transcendent encounter. God instructed her in a dream to wait for the first woman who came out from the baptistery after being baptized and to ask her to make the sign of the cross over the cancer. Innocentia did so and was immediately cured. Her physician later confirmed the disappearance of the cancer, but she mostly kept silent about the experience.

When Augustine heard that she had been healed, he reprimanded her for not sharing the experience widely. He then had her recount the story to her friends in Augustine's presence. As Augustine wrote, "I made her tell how the whole thing happened, from beginning to end, while the other women listened in great astonishment, and glorified God."[43]

Many of the stories of wonder Augustine recounted centered on the shrine of St. Stephen situated at his church at Hippo. Accounts of mystical experiences, such as visions and all kinds of other miracles, were reported from shrines throughout the many centuries of the Church.

Like Augustine, Saint Gregory, bishop of Tours, recounted the many miracles and visionary experiences that happened at the

43. Augustine of Hippo, *City of God* (Edinburgh, 1871), 489.

shrine of St. Martin of Tours and throughout Gaul, the area that is now France.

Visionary mystical experiences were common in Gaul through the eighth century, not just in saints' lives but among ordinary people. Isabel Moreira's scholarly book *Dreams, Visions, and Spiritual Authority in Merovingian Gaul* documents the prevalence of visions in this era. She writes, "A strong tradition of unrestricted access to the supernatural through dreams and visions persisted into the early middle ages...."[44] She also notes that more and more emphasis was placed on the mystical visions of holy people and saints. As she states clearly, "By the high middle ages, visionary literature and dream narratives were at the heart of the Christian tradition."[45] In Gaul, she says, "The texts are alive with humble, dirty and rascally inhabitants of Gaul who were apparently ennobled by divine favor."[46]

Mystical visions could turn a sinner back to God's love, accompany the sick on their road of healing, and assure those in turmoil of his comfort. They were widespread through the Middle Ages.

The documentation was often thorough, especially during the period of 1050 to 1350. Clerics took depositions, often with intense cross-examination, of those who claimed healings and those who witnessed them. Moreover, scholars have discovered thousands of these depositions. They clearly show the spirituality, and even the mysticism, of common people.

Those healed frequently saw visions, often of light or a saint, at the time of their healings. Sometimes visions instructed individuals to go to a shrine or church for healing, as in the case of Innocentia. At times groups of people shared a mystical experience at the time of healing. A light would often invade the church where scores of sick

---

44. Isabel Moreira, *Dreams, Visions, and Spiritual Authority in Merovingian Gaul* (Ithaca: Cornell University Press, 2000), 15.

45. Ibid., 3.

46. Ibid., 15.

and injured would be sleeping and praying, followed by healings and individual holy visions of those being healed.[47] Medievalist Ward asserts there are no signs of fraud in the texts that document these wonders, although looking back through the centuries we cannot say what actually occurred. As she tells it, "all that can be said is that here events that caused wonder and awe and were interpreted...as signs of the action of God in human affairs."[48] She reiterates this point in the concluding remarks to her book:

> Perhaps the first conclusion that can be drawn is that the records of miracles in the Middle Ages are not merely bizarre sidelights to the religion of the period. They provide, rather, a way to approach the ordinary day-to-day life of men and women in all kinds of situations and in all ranks of society, and serious historians must take them into consideration.[49]

When today's theologians and spiritual writers begin to process these accounts, it will mean a Copernican revolution in our understanding of spirituality. They will find that mystical encounter was not restricted to a privileged few, but widespread among average people. The door will open wide for ordinary people today to touch the holy mystery of God's manifestation among us, just as the earlier generations of mystics did.

Another way our ancestors in faith passed stories of the wondrous down to us is in the lives of the saints. The original sources on saints' lives abound with mystical experiences, visionary and otherwise. For instance, Paulinus, who wrote the first life of Saint Ambrose, the eloquent bishop and preacher of Milan whom he knew well, tells of a mystical experience he personally witnessed. He writes that a few days before he was confined to his couch, in his final illness:

---

47. André Vauchez, *La Sainteté en Occident aux derniers siècles du Moyen-Age. D'après les procès de canonisacion et les documents hagiographiques* (Rome: Ecole Française de Rome, 1981; Paris: Diffusion de Boccard, 1988), 18–23.

48. Ward, 215–16.

49. Ibid., 214.

when he was dictating the forty-third psalm, with me carefully taking it down, a fire like a small shield suddenly covered his head, and little by little entered his mouth, just as a person enters his home. After this, his face turned white as snow, but soon regained its usual appearance....I, you may be sure, straightway reported what I had seen to the honorable deacon Castus, under whose care I was then living. But he, filled with the grace of God, pointed out to me from the passage of the Acts of the Apostles that I had seen in the bishop the coming of the Holy Spirit.[50]

In modern times scholars often dismiss such spiritual experiences as invented additions to saints' lives. Now that more and more of the depositions of ordinary people describing cures and visions are studied, we find these mystical touches in the midst of people's daily life, and it becomes harder to dismiss these tales of wonder as simple fiction.

The more we study, the more we find many great thinkers and theologians possessed the fervent heart of mystics in their private life. Bernard Gui, in his eloquently written life of Thomas Aquinas, suggested every Mass was a mystical experience for Thomas. During Mass he "was utterly absorbed in the mystery, and his face ran with tears."[51] He often prayed with tears, sighs, and great fervor seeking inward stirring of the Spirit on what to write or preach.[52] Despite his great intellect, he possessed a simple human heart as focused on God's love as a needle is to a magnet. The portrait Gui gives us for Thomas is backed up by Thomas' own words. In his *Commentary on the Sentences*, he speaks of how prayer can engage the emotions and the body. He advocates praying aloud at times as part of our devotions:

---

50. Paulinus, *The Life of Ambrose*, found in *Early Christian Biographies*, trans. Roy J. Deferrari (Washington, DC: Catholic University of America Press, 1952), 59.

51. Bernard Gui, *The Life of St. Thomas: Biographical Documents* (Baltimore: Helicon Press, 1959), 37.

52. Ibid., 43, 38, 39, 46.

First, (praying aloud) is a way in which we can stir ourselves with our words to pray with devotion. Secondly, praying aloud can keep our attention from wandering, because we can concentrate better if we support our feelings with words when we pray...when our mind is kindled by devotion as we pray, we break out spontaneously into weeping and sighing and cries of jubilation and other such noises...we have to serve the God to whom we offer reverence in prayer not only with our minds, but also with our bodies.[53]

In addition to times of prayer, mystical experiences recorded in the past often involved nature. Nature was transfigured and nature became an emblem of the divine. Most of us know that nature played a great role in the lives of Saint Francis and the early Franciscans, but Protestants also knew the mysticism of nature. Jonathan Edwards wrote:

...there seemed to be...(an) appearance of divine glory, in almost everything. God's excellency, his wisdom, his purity and love, seemed to appear in everything; in the sun, and moon, and stars; in the clouds and blue sky; in the grass, flowers, trees; in the water, and all nature; which used greatly to fix my mind. I often used to...behold the sweet glory of God in these things....[54]

Practical Steps

Our ancestors in faith saw everything as both miracle and natural at the same time. They had what Benedicta Ward calls a more subtle understanding than we possess. Natural causes, not yet seen, often played a role. In a miracle, God let those natural causes unfold in an

53. Simon Tugwell, ed. *Albert and Thomas: Selected Writings (Classics of Western Spirituality)* (New York: Paulist Press, 1988), 380.

54. Michael J. McClymond, *Encounters with God: An Approach to the Theology of Jonathan Edwards* (New York: Oxford University Press, 1998), 25.

extraordinary way. Miracles were not miracles because God acted in them and nowhere else. The idea that miracles are a breaking of natural law is only a modern one. Before, it was expected that unseen causes, by the touch of God, were manifested in miracles. These events helped everyone see the wondrous that was in everything.

An experience doesn't have to be stupendous to be wondrous.

I remember one fall I had a bad case of writer's block. I was contracted to write a book; the deadline loomed, but the words would simply not come. I drew a blank. How could I possibly finish a manuscript when I felt a wall within me blocking off ideas?

Deacon Herrmann, who works with me, suggested we go for a ride to nearby Pine Mountain. At first, I couldn't enjoy the brilliant fall scenery because my mind stayed stuck in fear of not having enough ideas to finish the book. We drove on up to Warm Springs, GA, a quaint town north of Pine Mountain, where we had a delicious barbeque lunch. On the way back home I finally found myself noticing the scenery. The wonder of the bright golds and reds of the leaves sank into my soul. For a while, I stopped thinking about the book.

We drove to Dowdell's Knob, a famous lookout over the Pine Mountain Valley, and I looked out at the broad, expansive landscape of the valley. *Something this beautiful shows there has to be a God*, I thought. In the midst of the wonder, the Spirit stirred my heart.

Writing about God is not nearly as important as tasting of his nearness. I realized how much everyday joy and peace I had abandoned just to write the book. The book had taken me over, and I was reminded once again that we are human beings, not human doings, and I had been spending far too much time doing than being lately. It was far more important for me to experience God and the wonder of his world than write about God.

This epiphany helped me see that I needed to take time just to live, time for more prayer, time for walks and fresh air. For a few days, I didn't think about the writing project. When I finally started writing my book again, I didn't let it take me over. I spent less time on it and more time living. However, the ideas and words overflowed like a fountain, and my writing was far richer than before. Moreover, the book came so easily that I finished it a month ahead of the deadline.

That day on the mountain was a miracle for me. No angels sang, no heavenly pictures passed before my eyes, but the still, small voice of God taught me a lesson that changed my life forever. Have there been miracles like that in your own life? Times of sudden and sacred insight that helped shape your life?

▶ Think about such times in your past, and write up the experience in your journal.

Scripture Reflection

"And if I have prophetic powers, and understand all mysteries and all knowledge, and if I have all faith, so as to remove mountains, but do not have love, I am nothing."

• *1 CORINTHIANS 13:2*

The test of any spiritual experience is if it helps us love our neighbor better and love God better. In the midst of our seeking God's presence and God's touches, our hearts should be centered on returning the love given to us, not thinking of spiritual experiences as merit badges. When God loves us, he goes out of himself, and he means for that same love that fills us to pour out of us, to carry us beyond ourselves.

Guided Meditation

Take time to grow still. Notice your breathing in and your breathing out. Each time you exhale, breathe out negativity. Each time you inhale, breathe in the restorative presence of God.

Let the stillness sweep over you as you sink deeper and deeper into the love of God.

Remember some of the miracles of the Bible, such as Lazarus raised up by Jesus or the healing of the man born blind. Think over some of the wondrous manifestations in Scripture, such as the angels appearing to the shepherds at the nativity scene, the mountain of transfiguration, the descent of the Holy Spirit at Christ's baptism, or the coming of the Spirit at baptism. Envision these scenes vividly as though you were there.

Recall some of the miracles and wonder in your own life—times the sacred burst into your life.

Imagine you are in a boat, resting on a mattress with your neck and head on a large pillow, as it drifts down a slow-moving stream. You hear the water splash by the side of the boat, easing you, relaxing you. The more the boat moves down the stream, the deeper you drift into a deep peacefulness. The majesty of God's creation enchants you. You see a bright blue, cloudless sky. The sunlight beams down on you, warming you, penetrating the deepest part of your being. This is not ordinary sunlight; it is the sunlight of God's own love. You see waves of grain blown by a gentle wind on both banks. You realize that you are in the midst of a miracle: God's own creation. Just continue to flow down the stream till you rest deeply in the marvelous peace of God.

CHAPTER 7

Inner Cleansing

People find it so easy to think that the great "lovers of God" through the centuries just experienced one spiritual delight after another, but, as Evelyn Underhill puts it, "Willingly and perpetually, they prayed from within the Cross, shared the agony, darkness, loneliness of the Cross..."[55]

When we let God's love move within us, opening the doors of our hearts to his tender Spirit, we begin to see the falsities in our lives. It is so easy to believe we can manage our lives and our world, keep fear and anguish at bay, control our existence. It is also easy to have a false face with which we meet the world, one that seemingly has no wrinkles, no scars, is in charge, and expresses no cry for help or nurture. In short, the easy path in today's world is to live in denial.

The media tell us that the latest facial formula or the right exercise

---

55. Underhill, 87.

machine will put smiles on our faces; if we purchase just the right car, perfect joy is ours.

As we bask in the love of God, we find it harder to keep up such pretense, either to others or to ourselves. Our world ceases to seem so manageable, and we are forced to look at the raw pain in our lives and the raw pain in the world. We realize how little in control we really are. It is then we enter what the mystics have called purgation. In this process of purgation, we are radically rearranged. We undergo the breakup of our old personal universe, in order that we may let it go and receive it back as a new creation.

We begin to relinquish attachments to things, position, false pleasures; we fall back on our own helplessness and then turn to God in that helplessness. God strips us of what is false to make room for new growth, just as a gardener prunes a bush. This purging hurts. God weans us, at times gently and at times roughly, from depending on anything but the one love that powers the sun and the stars and upholds the universe. When we go through this purgation, it may even seem at times that God has abandoned us. As the Dutch mystic Blessed John of Ruysbroeck puts it, "God will hide himself and withdraw his hand, placing between himself and you a darkness which you will not be able to see through. You will then lament, moan, and groan like a poor abandoned exile." However, Ruysbroeck goes on to tell us there is no need for despair: "If God has hidden himself from your sight, you are nevertheless not hidden from him, for he lives within you and has left the gift of his mirror and image, namely, his Son Jesus Christ, your Bridegroom."[56]

God calls us at such times to a stark trust and dependence on him. Many spiritual authors have recommended that in those times we pray the lament sections of the Psalms, such as Psalm 44:

> Rouse yourself! Why do you sleep, O Lord?
>   Awake, do not cast us off forever!
> Why do you hide your face?

---

56. Fanning, 115.

Why do you forget our affliction and oppression?
For we sink down to the dust;
   our bodies cling to the ground.
Rise up, come to our help.
Redeem us for the sake of your steadfast love.

                         • *PSALM 44:23–26*

JACK'S STORY

Jack always wanted to serve the Church. When he was little, Mass enthralled him. At age five, he would take time off from playing cowboy to make a small altar out of a box and pretend to be the priest celebrating Mass. At age nine, he graduated from "playing priest" to volunteering as an altar server for his parish. It overjoyed him to be a helper in worship.

When he graduated from high school, he swallowed hard and filled out the application for the priesthood in his diocese. On one hand, he felt a strong yearning to publicly be in ministry; on the other, his stomach tightened at the thought of all he would have to give up. You see, there was a young woman named Clare in his life. He had dated her throughout his senior year of high school. He was richly and madly in love, yet he felt a nearly irresistible tug to serve God by becoming the minister he dreamed of being when he played Church with his makeshift altar as a child.

In late August, one week before he was to enter the seminary, the calling to love a woman and have a family seemed the greater call. His stomach churning with anxiety, he called his vocations director and told him of his changed plans. He felt right with his decision. Two years later, he married Clare. He went on to get his MBA and became a highly successful, near wealthy, businessperson. He and Clare raised three sons.

To his delight, Jack found he could take an active role in ministry as a layperson. He lectored at Mass on Sundays; he headed up his parish's successful evangelism effort. He possessed an innate sense of how to be compassionate and pastoral with people. Yet he yearned for more.

His gifts in ministry had long caught the eye of his pastor. One Tuesday the pastor invited him to his rectory office for a chat. His pastor smiled broadly and got right to the point. "It's obvious to me and so many others in this parish that you seem to have a special calling. I wonder if it isn't time now to begin a process that will lead to your ordination. You could be of even more help to me and the Church."

The pastor's words left Jack near speechless. *How could I be ordained?* he thought; *after all, I am married.*

Then the answer came. The pastor continued, "Our diocese will be beginning a new class of permanent deacons. As you probably know, deacons are ordained, usually married, clergy who can preach, marry, baptize, assist at Mass, and live out the calling to be a servant."

Every word his pastor uttered resonated deep within Jack. Perhaps this had been his calling all along. His pastor's words felt like they were calling to his deepest self, and he said yes to a call that had been on his mind from the time he was little.

Jack began the long education and discernment process of becoming a deacon. As a deacon candidate he now attended the same seminary he had once considered entering to study for priesthood as a young man. Learning more fully about Scripture and pastoral ministry thrilled him. He and his fellow deacon candidates made yearly retreats in which the retreat leaders introduced them to contemplative prayer and meditations. Several of his professors led the group in guided meditations, a way of prayer he found rich and soul filling.

In his daydreams he could see himself preaching, helping lead worship, serving the poorest of the poor—in short, waiting on tables as a servant, which is the call of a deacon. Then something frightening happened at the beginning of his last year of training. The thrill left his considerations of becoming a deacon. As the scenes of serving as a deacon passed through his mind, now he felt nothing. It no longer excited him. Even worse, his prayer and devotional times, which at the start of his formation had seemed so sweet, now seemed bland. He began asking himself, *Is all this time and effort just a big waste?* He thought of all the additional time serving as a deacon would take from his already busy life. God seemed far away; Mass felt boring. He felt empty.

This was not what was supposed to happen, he thought. How could he serve as a minister now that he was numbed to the realities of his faith? He struggled mightily.

The calendar kept moving forward to ordination day. The time came for the group's final canonical retreat just before ordination. On this retreat, the candidates were to say a final yes or no to becoming deacons. The diocese held the retreat at a Benedictine monastery within the diocese. As Jack began the retreat, he felt desperate. His stomach churned just the same as it had when he almost studied for the priesthood. Surely God had not led him this far to abandon him.

In his down time from the retreat, he would listen to the monks chant the Psalms as part of their daily prayer. The Psalms that spoke of being abandoned by God, alone and helpless, resounded in his soul. Those Psalms described how he felt.

He finally poured out his emotions to an especially holy monk at the monastery. Tears streamed out of his eyes as he told the monk of his predicament. The gentle monk listened with a wide and caring heart.

The monk told him, "Sometimes God hides that we may seek him for himself. God's seeming disappearance may just be a way of drawing you closer to himself, making sure you become a deacon for the right reasons. You have had your mind fixed on the joys of ministry, on scenes of being dressed in vestments leading worship. Perhaps what God is doing is saying that he wants you for more than what you can do for him, more than outward things. He wants you to love him for himself, not because of the excitement of ministry. He wants you depending on him rather than your skills as a minister or a businessperson." The monk finished by reading these words from the great Spanish mystic John of the Cross: "O guiding night! O night more lovely than the dawn! O night that has united the lover with his beloved, Transforming the beloved in her lover."[57]

When Jack went back to his room, a sweet sense of God's nearness filled him. He prayed, "O God, you are dear to me, dearer than ministry, dearer to me than my work. It's good to let go of my focus on my role and collapse in the arms of your love."

In sensing God in a deeper way, he felt a renewed call to ministry and two weeks later found himself lying face down in the cathedral as the choir sang the Litany of the Saints at his ordination. Over the next few months, he felt God's abiding love in the recesses of his soul. God was now more than a ministry coordinator; God was truly his Beloved.

As the years passed, there would be other times when God seemed absent. Old lessons at times had to be learned afresh on a deeper level. Now though, he had an understanding of why God seemed to disappear. In this work of cleansing, God was stripping away the false, cutting through the counterfeit and renewing Jack's core. God was knitting his heart to Jack's.

Johann Arndt, the German Lutheran mystic, reminds us that "when God's help appears to be withdrawn, we must remember that God is never far from us. Therefore, have faith and be patient. God has foreseen our situation and will bring about our redemption."[58]

---

57. Kieran Kavanaugh, ed., *John of the Cross: Selected Writings* (New York: Paulist Press, 1988), 55.

58. Arndt, 217.

We go through a process of simplification and self-surrender. The Holy Spirit flows downhill, like water to the lowest valley, not uphill to the heights. Our journey into God's love involves lament, telling him of our sorrow, need, and misery, that he may refashion us to be lovers of God and all God's creation.

In addition, even during the facing of our pain and the world's pain, we can experience an inflow of the holy that makes even the times of having falsity stripped away from us sweet.

When God seems to disappear, when we no longer feel his closeness, when we encounter these times of spiritual "dryness," our first impulse may be to despair. However, through that very dryness God may be calling us into a richer communion. Actually, our prayer during this time may be the best prayer we have prayed, for we are praying, not for the feeling of consolation, but because we love God and are faithful in prayer even when we don't feel anything. We are learning, as Saint Teresa of Avila puts it, "to seek the God of consolations and not the consolations of God."[59] God is busy purifying our love.

Imagine you are praying at night in a chapel illuminated by one candle. Someone slips in and turns the bright overhead lights on. You are blinded until your eyes adjust. So it is with God. When his light bursts out around us, we are blinded by it until we inwardly adjust to it. As George Fox, founder of the Quakers, reminds us, "the same light that shows us our sin heals us."

Practical Steps

Old Testament scholar Walter Brueggemann tells us that "in our consumer culture negative emotion isn't actively denied, instead it is passively ignored, like an unintelligible language of gibberish."[60] The

---

59. Quoted in Thomas H. Green SJ, *When the Well Runs Dry* (Notre Dame, IN: Ave Maria Press), 94.

60. Walter Brueggemann, *The Psalmist's Cry: Scripts for Embracing Lament* (Kansas City: The House Studio, 2010), 38.

media subtly school us to ignore pain by bombarding us with images of people who overcome discomfort by acquiring the latest gadget, game, jeans, or car.

▶ Think of some ways you might be denying your own negative emotions. What would happen if you accessed some of that pain? What would it be like to pour out our feelings of abandonment to God?

▶ Journal a few minutes on this topic.

Scripture Reflection

The Old Testament, in Jeremiah 18:1–6, presents us with an excellent example in the story of the potter molding his clay. In the midst of the times when the unmanageability of our world weighs us down and tightens our insides, the image of God shaping us can liberate us.

> The word that came to Jeremiah from the Lord: "Come, go down to the potter's house, and there I will let you hear my words." So I went down to the potter's house, and there he was working at his wheel. The vessel he was making of clay was spoiled in the potter's hand, and he reworked it into another vessel, as seemed good to him.
>
> Then the word of the Lord came to me: Can I not do with you, O house of Israel, just as this potter has done? says the Lord. Just like the clay in the potter's hand, so are you in my hand, O house of Israel. • *JEREMIAH 18:1–6*

This originally meant that Israel had turned out badly and was now being broken and reshaped by Yahweh. We can apply this same passage to ourselves. Only the potter knows the shape of the vase he is molding from the moist clay. We don't know yet fully how God is molding us, what shape we will be. We are just clay in his hands. What we can do, however, is relinquish our life to his hands and trust that the potter knows what he is doing.

Guided Meditation

Begin to slow down; perhaps put on some stilling, calming music, such as Gregorian chant or sounds of nature. Let the great stillness flow over you.

God is near. He surrounds you.

Jesus stands beside you and places his hand on your shoulders. It is safe, so very safe to be here with Jesus. It's easy at such a time to feel your feelings of abandonment, isolation, dryness.

The holy light that surrounds Jesus now surrounds you. It pours over you, calms you, and warms you. Sense the light absorbing your negative emotions.

You breathe in the light. It fills you from the top of your head to the bottom of your feet. As you feel safe and comfortable, let words that describe your unprocessed pain flow out of you in a prayer to Jesus who is now so gently comforting you.

CHAPTER 8

How God Can Change Us Over a Lifetime

God's grace can transform us, imbue us with his presence, and help us become the people he intended us to be from all eternity. From the moment of conception, he has built into us an affinity for that grace. We were built with an inclination toward him, built for him to transform us. This affinity is the image of God within, as writers through the centuries tell us. His freely given grace can work a wonder throughout our entire being, making us his new creation, his own sons and daughters.

❧ CHARLES' STORY

Charles was the youngest of four brothers. His father, a retired army sergeant who supported his family through teaching

ROTC at a local high school, struggled with alcoholism. When sober, he was a strong, caring father. When he drank, however, he wielded words like weapons, occasionally using his fists.

Charles said his father, when he was drinking, was a "rageaholic." His mother cowered when his father ranted; Charles had no one to protect him. It seemed that the smallest thing could set off a stream of verbal abuse. If a hair was misplaced on his head, his father would blow up. When Charles was ten, his father caught him with his shirttail out. "You're a lazy, worthless excuse for a son. I wish you had never been born," his father thundered, knocking him up against a wall with one hand and slapping him with the other. Charles knew if he said a single word in his own defense, it would only make matters worse.

Despite this, Charles succeeded at school and at sports, becoming the best pitcher in the last ten years of his little league team. When sober, his dad showed immense pride in his son, bragging about him with his coworkers; while drinking, he forgot all that was good about his son.

Charles lived constantly with anxiety. Happy, carefree moments could never be fully enjoyed for fear of the tumult that might lie ahead. And Charles blamed himself. Surely he had a profound defect in his soul to so enrage his father.

In high school, Charles dated regularly. He loved the physical affirmation that came from his arm wrapped around a girl, but he could never trust that affirmation fully. He easily found defects and faults with the girls he dated, just as his father found defects in him. He never succeeded at a close, steady relationship. He would simply leave those relationships without a word, often deeply wounding the young women.

An academic scholarship to a distant college took him away from the rage that filled his home. He majored in history, with an emphasis on medieval history. The whole medieval period with all its mystery and wonder became a calm respite to the uncertainty he felt inside.

He felt there was, as he described it, "a hole in his soul." He hoped just the right woman would meet his standards, but one never came along. When he thought of his future, it seemed barren to him. He pictured himself teaching history in college, all alone, with no closeness to anyone. He knew he carried the tumult of his home in his soul, and he didn't know how to expunge it.

Raised Catholic, he still attended Mass, and he found the sacred hour an oasis from his inner turmoil. Charles' interest in medievalism led him to read the early stories of the life of Saint Francis. The personality of Francis entranced him. The very language of those early biographies carried a wonder and warmth that bathed him in peace. He wanted to meet God in bold encounter like Francis. He yearned for a simple, trusting heart like Francis'. As he read on, he saw Francis' closeness to God and his closeness to people: two things Charles wanted in his own life. He perceived there was more, much more, to the encounter with God than he ever dared dream.

Now he wondered how to draw close to God like Francis. He knew, as with Francis, that central to that closeness was taking Jesus into the center of his heart, letting the words of the Gospels enrich his heart. Prayer played a central role too. Prayer united Francis' heart to Jesus' heart.

Charles began a serious adult prayer life. He saw how Francis talked to God intimately as a friend.

He had read *The Way of the Pilgrim*, the nineteenth-century Russian story of how repeating simple prayers around the name of Jesus warmed and remade the heart. Charles set up a makeshift altar in his dorm room with a candle and a picture of Jesus. Sitting on the floor, his back against the wall, he began repeating the name of Jesus. Soon his heart settled down. He sensed something rumbling in his soul but, at this point, did not experience the closeness of God. He became faithful in his praying, taking as much as an hour or more a day in his prayer corner.

Then one day he found his prayer repeating in his soul without consciously willing it as he went about his everyday activities. Then another day, soon after this, he felt a warmth radiate throughout his soul and body, a radiance that could be nothing less than the presence of Jesus. He found this warmth would come and go throughout his daily activity.

His hour of prayer at night took on new depths. In the stillness, he found memories of his father's abuse emerge in painful detail that grabbed at his gut. He re-experienced the horror, but this time around, it was different. His gentle Jesus prayer, his waiting before God in the stillness, anchored him in God's love. This time when he relived the experiences he was not alone; he relived them with his head resting on the bosom of God.

As the months went on, there seemed to be an endless stream of memories. Slowly and carefully as he opened himself up to divine love, the sting began to leave those memories. They seemed more distant now. He also turned over in his mind some of his dating relationships, remembering how he coldly locked young women out of his life when he witnessed their imperfections. He could now feel the hurt that they felt. He yearned to love with the same love that now gripped his soul.

Gradually, he began more mature dating relationships. He went out with a young woman named Jane and fell into a solid, sustaining relationship with her. They thought of marriage. Even though he was ready to buy an engagement ring, Charles had an inner feeling that marriage was not for him. He felt a clear calling from God to a lasting relationship, not with a woman, but with the Church. He felt God summoning him to the priesthood.

Telling Jane of his new calling was difficult. She fumed for weeks, but they continued to be friends. She finally agreed that the priesthood was his vocation, and they remained close friends. She and her new husband came to his ordination seven years later.

As he went through seminary, Charles' relationship with God developed further. On a retreat for the seminarians, he discovered imaginative meditation. His prayer times changed from being times of inward healing to being times when a bright newness infused his soul. He could sense God's presence in the everyday world around him. He reached out to the poor, the marginalized, with the same love with which God loved him.

Charles is in his fifties now, and God still gently abides in his soul. He says he is aware of God constantly in all his wondrous mystery. His simple sermons, imbued with the Divine Presence, leave many in tears at the tenderness of God's love. His voice and his mannerisms all hint at a love that is far greater than us. People say they feel God by being near him. Christians from far away and from other faith expressions come to him for counseling. Many leave saying they felt immersed in love just through his presence.

Repentance and inner cleansing usually characterize first stages on our progress into God's love. Later, in the illuminative stage, there is a deepening, an enlarging, of our hearts. But that growth "is punctuated by crises in which growth appears to have come to a stop for a time; old battles have to be refought and old experiences relived at a deeper level."[61] In the illuminative way, the moral dimensions of our lives blossom. We begin to reach out and love from our authentic self in all areas of our lives.

The final stage of development in the mystical life is the unitive stage. We don't arrive at full unity with God overnight. It takes time: time to empty out our negative and conflicted emotions, our resentments, our sin, any remaining resistance to God; time to become like

---

61. Cheslyn Jones, Geoffrey Wainwright, Edward Yarnold, *The Study of Spirituality* (New York: Oxford University Press, 1986), 566

the one who so loves us; time to grow from a self-centered universe to a God-centered universe.

We can taste only partially in this life the completed union with God, which comes only in glory through the beatific vision. But there are points in our lives, even in the very beginning, when we can perceive the intimate communications of his tender love.

The unitive state of mystical development is reached when we have been changed from an anxiety-centered existence to a peace-centered existence. In this stage, we have a foretaste of the beatific vision. Alexander Maclaren describes this state beautifully when he writes:

> Between him and them there is a communion of love, a union of life, and a consequent reciprocal knowledge, which transcends the closest intimacies of earthly life, and finds its only analogue in that deep and mysterious oneness which subsists between the Father...and the only begotten Son...[62]

For Maclaren our hearts blend with Christ's heart. He says that even in the beginning of our journey there can be times when "we touch the warm, throbbing heart of our Friend, who lives forever, and forever is near us."[63] He beautifully captures the unity between us and Christ, saying, "[Christ] can lay his hand upon your spirit's hand. He can flash light into your spirit's eye from his eye. He can put breath and eloquence into your spirit's lips from his lips, and his heart beating against yours can transfuse—if I may so say—into you his own lifeblood."[64]

---

62. Alexander Maclaren, *Expositions of Holy Scripture: St John Ch. I to XIV* (Christian Classics Ethereal Library), www.ccel.org/ccel/maclaren/john1.ii.xliii.html, accessed September 27, 2011.

63. Alexander Maclaren, *The Gospel According to St. John, Vol. 3* (New York: A.C. Armstrong and Son, 1908), 41.

64. Alexander Maclaren, *The Second Book of Kings From Chap. VIII* (New York: A.C. Armstrong and Son), 28.

Despite this unity, we do not cease to be our unique selves. Maclaren explains that this union with God "does not destroy, but heightens, my individuality. I am more and not less myself because 'I live, yet not I, but Christ liveth in me.'"[65]

Some mystics, like Saint Bernard of Clairvaux, have described this unity as a spiritual marriage between God and the soul. Among Eastern Christians, this process of transformation is often called deification—becoming like God. Nevertheless, the otherness of God is retained. God is near, but he is also always other, and we never cease to be his creatures. Gottfried Arnold, a Lutheran Pietist, writes, "Such love gains its end only in heaven, but it can achieve ecstatic insights while on earth, although its ultimate goal here is peace and joy in the Holy Spirit."[66]

Contemplating God over time changes not only our souls, but our bodies and brains as well. Andrew Newberg, a research neurologist at the University of Pennsylvania, has done clinical studies over a number of years of people who pray and meditate on God, often for a lifetime. He writes:

> If you contemplate God long enough, something surprising happens in the brain. Neural functioning begins to change. Different circuits become activated, while others become deactivated. New dendrites are formed, new synaptic connections are made, and the brain becomes more sensitive to subtle realms of experience.[67]

According to Newberg, spiritual practices positively affect the functioning of the brain and increase bodily and mental health. Contemplation of God over the years makes enduring changes to our brains, affecting those parts of the brain that regulate moods and form our very concepts of self.

---

65. Maclaren, *St. John, Vol. 3*, 218.

66. Peter C. Erb, ed., *The Pietists: Selected Writings* (New York: Paulist Press, 1983), 13.

67. Andrew Newberg, *How God Changes Your Brain* (New York: Ballantine Books, 2009), 13.

Furthermore, spiritual practice over the years "specifically enhances social awareness and empathy, while subduing destructive feelings and emotions," he says. He suggests that spiritual practice could slow down the effects of diseases such as Alzheimer's and Parkinson's. Spiritual practice over a lifetime "will bring permanent changes to the brain,"[68] he concludes.

Practical Steps

▶ Pick a spot in your house to use to pray or meditate daily. Perhaps put up some sacred pictures, leave a copy of the Bible there, and perhaps keep a vigil candle in the space.

▶ Take time each day, preferably the same time every day, for sacred practice, Scripture reading, and reflection.

Scripture Reflection

But thanks be to God, who in Christ always leads us in triumphal procession, and through us spreads in every place the fragrance that comes from knowing him. For we are the aroma of Christ to God among those who are being saved and among those who are perishing; to the one a fragrance from death to death, to the other a fragrance from life to life. Who is sufficient for these things? For we are not peddlers of God's word like so many; but in Christ we speak as persons of sincerity, as persons sent from God and standing in his presence.   • *2 CORINTHIANS 2:14‒17*

God intends for us who are sent forth to not only speak of him, but to become his very fragrance. He wants us to be so close to him that others taste of his presence just being around us.

Such ability to convey his nearness does not happen in an instant; it takes time. It is a process and it takes a lifetime. Let us forever

---

68. Ibid., 48.

contemplate God, so that as time passes we become like the one we contemplate.

Guided Meditation

Let the quiet overtake you. Sink into the holy presence. Unwind in the stillness. Feel the warmth of God's love relaxing your arms, your face, your neck and shoulder.

The healing warmth passes into the muscles of your chest, your back, your stomach. Your legs grow greatly relaxed as the healing warmth flows into your thighs and calves.

Stay in the peacefulness, slowly repeating Jesus' name: Jesus, Lord Jesus.

Think back over some of the times you have felt God's love change you, helped you face sorrow, guilt or worry with grace and peace.

Remember some of the times God's nearness cleansed you, emptying you out of negativity and replacing that negativity with love.

Remember some of the times God invaded you with a bright newness, conveying without words his wondrous mystery to your soul.

Now picture what your life would be like if God were as close as you wanted him to be, if you loved others with the same love with which God loves you.

Say a prayer in your own words, asking God to speed you along the journey of closeness to him, your fellow humans and all creation.

CHAPTER 9

Imaginative Meditation

A Doorway into the Heart of God

In meditation, we take time to allow God to penetrate our souls. Sixteenth-century Catholic priest and spiritual writer Saint Francis de Sales defines meditation as a "reflection in great detail, point by point, on those things which are capable of touching our hearts."[69]

Nineteenth-century Baptist Bible expositor Alexander Maclaren has this to say about meditation:

> You must go into the depths of God through Christ. You must go into the depths of your own souls through him. You must become accustomed to withdraw yourselves from spreading

---

69. Wendy M. Wright, ed., *Francis de Sales: Essential Writings* (New York: Crossroads Publishing Company, 1994), 146.

yourselves out…and live alone with Jesus, 'in the secret place of the Most High.'[70]

As toddlers, before we know words we know the language of imagination. In adulthood, imagination remains the language of the unconscious. Imagination can fill us with a sense of deep-down knowing. Advertisers know this: they realize that imagination is the fastest route to our interior being. Imagination, symbols, and drama also greet us in most church services. Prayer that reaches below the surface into our inner core that makes us who we are must be imaginative. Prayer that uses imagination can lodge in our inner recesses where our identity and our behavior are determined. As theologian Kathleen Fischer states it, "The imagination enables us to live in multi-leveled, multi-colored truth, and to receive the truth which is pervaded by mist and mystery."[71] Or as Avery Dulles S.J. writes, revelation "is mediated through symbol—that is to say, through an externally perceived sign that works mysteriously on the human consciousness so as to suggest more than it can clearly describe or define."[72]

When you pray, you make use of the imagination, though often without fully realizing it. The Stations of the Cross, the Rosary and so many other ways of praying are based on the imagination, which is why they contain so much power to change us. In Protestant worship, hymns that paint vivid pictures are sung in worship. Christian mysticism thrives on holy imagination. Most forms of meditation use the imagination. Learning imaginative prayer can brighten our lives and lead us right into the lap of God.

Our consciousness has been described as an iceberg with the smallest part of the ice breaking the surface. The ice that breaks the

---

70. Alexander Maclaren, *The Gospel of John Chapters IX–XIV* (New York: A.C. Armstrong and Son, 1908), 29.

71. Kathleen R. Fischer, *The Inner Rainbow: The Imagination in Christian Life* (New York: Paulist Press, 1983), 7.

72. Avery Dulles, "The Symbolic Structure of Revelation," *Theological Studies 41/1* (March 1980), 55–56.

surface and protrudes above the water is our surface consciousness. The greater part, which is below the conscious level, is the unconscious. Here reside the wondrous sights and sounds and smells of childhood and our early discovery of the world. Here reside our traumas, our hurts. Here we find the parts of us we are ashamed of, hidden, at times even walled off, far below the surface.

To fully become who God intended us to be, that bright, special creation of his, we need to let God below the surface. Prayer using the imagination is a major way we let God into these subterranean depths.

Jesus' words use imagination to enchant the listener into the reality of the kingdom. New Testament scholar Amos Wilder writes of Jesus, "The hearer not only learns about that reality, he participates in it. He is invaded by it….Jesus' speech had the character not of instruction and ideas but of compelling imagination, a spell, a transformation."[73]

The importance of using our imaginations in prayer is one reason I have provided guided meditation throughout this book. Guided imaginative meditations, in which we enter imaginatively into Scriptural scenes or other holy scenes, played a major role in disposing people for the encounter with God from the Hebrew Scriptures, through the history of the Church until our own day. Psalm 23 is a guided journey of meditation. The person who prays this prayer is taken into a peaceful meadow where the soul is restored, lingers beside restful waters, is anointed with oil.

The early Church fathers used imaginative prayer as part of their teaching. Cyril of Jerusalem led catechumens into holy imaginative scenes to prepare them for baptism. Ambrose included them in his sermons.

During the Age of Faith, Bonaventure, in his classic meditation the *Lignum Vitae, The Tree of Life*, and other mystical works, used the technique. In *The Tree of Life* he calls listeners on an experiential journey. His words grab for head and heart at the same time. He

---

73. Amos Niven Wilder, *Early Christian Rhetoric: The Language of the Gospel* (New York: Harper and Row, 1964), 84.

says, "Oh, if you could feel in some way the quality and intensity of that fire sent from heaven, the refreshing coolness that accompanied it, the consolation it imparted." In the section of the meditation that deals with Jesus' birth, he says, "embrace that divine manger; press your lips upon and kiss the boy's feet. Then in your mind keep the shepherd's watch....Receive the infant in your arms."[74] Guided meditations were used among religious and laity as well. As medievalist Despres' fascinating book on imaginative meditation in the late medieval period phrased it, these meditations "provided daily life with a conscious pattern of redemption."[75] Stories of saints and their miracles, laden with imaginative scenes, filled the ears of churchgoers. Priests and friars led congregations in these guided meditations. Imaginative prayer filled the devotional manuals. Experiences of the wondrous penetrated hearts.

Despres points out that these meditations reached deep within the laity.[76] Imagination and stories of God's calm and sweetness permeated the culture. Imaginative prayer, imaginative stories and plays unlocked the deeply sacramental and spontaneous religious imagination of the hearers and witnesses. It is also true that prayer without imagination existed, as in the case of the Eastern monks who emphasized the Jesus prayer, prayer of the heart, but even they prayed the Eastern liturgy, which was full rich, imaginative verbal icons. Both have a role. God, however, is always greater than our imagination.

These visionary meditations had profound life-changing effects on people. One expert, Paul Piehler, writes, "Medieval visionary allegory offers its readers participation in a process of psychic redemption closely resembling, though wider in scope than, modern psychotherapy."[77]

---

74. Bonaventure in Cousins, 36.

75. Denise Louise Despres, *Ghostly Sights: Visual Meditation in Late-Medieval Literature* (Norman, OK: Pilgrim Books, 1989), 26.

76. Ibid., 26.

77. Paul Piehler, *The Visionary Landscape: A Study in Medieval Allegory* (Edward Arnold Press, 1988), 3.

Our prayer lives are almost always supported in some way by the imagination. Certainly there are imageless, wordless, passive times in prayer, times of simply resting in God's love, experiencing him in depths beyond expression, contemplative prayer. However, even those moments are often triggered by imagination, as Saint Teresa of Avila, no stranger to speechless, imageless prayer, reminds us. Summarizing her attitude, Fischer says, "As the sixteenth-century mystic Teresa of Avila stresses, life's journey of prayer is long, and moments of imagelessness need to be understood and sustained in terms of the sacraments and other Christian symbols. Liturgy, Scripture, music, and art are essential to the total spiritual life of any Christian."[78]

I can say imaginative prayer has certainly enriched and altered my life. In the early 1980s I felt a strong stirring in my soul to write a book on emotional healing. This was a period in my life before my diagnosis of brain dysfunction. Despite not knowing why I had this array of problems I did not know the cause of, my life prospered. I had friends who helped me, to some degree, with the problems due to my cognitive deficits. These were the days before I had a personal computer, when the only means I thought I had of writing a book was by using a typewriter, ribbon and paper, a method that was immensely confusing to me because of my disability.

One night when praying, I pictured Jesus standing by me as I wrote the book on the typewriter. Then, in my imagination, I noticed the cassette recorder/player on the desk by the typewriter, and the inspiration came to me. *Why not record the book on tape and have it transcribed?* I tried this, sent it off to a service to have it transcribed and found a way around my disability. I prayed every night, imagining Jesus standing beside me as I dictated the book, light from his heart pouring over me as I recorded.

The next day at my desk dictating, the words flowed out of my mouth. I felt a radiant glowing in my heart. It was as though I was

---

78. Fischer, 70.

immersed in the light of God. Imaginative prayer had lessened my problems with attention and sequencing.

One night after I had prayed, again picturing Jesus, I fell into a deep sleep and dreamed a vivid dream. I dreamed of coming home one day and finding a note on the floor from my colleague Robert Herrmann; the note said a man from Harper and Row had called and was interested in publishing my book *Prayer that Heals Our Emotions*. In my waking state, I dismissed this as wishful thinking.

I self-published the book and soon had sold 15,000 books. I thought to myself, *If the book is popular enough to sell 15,000 copies, maybe it is good enough for me to send to Harper and Row*. I mailed off a copy with my address and phone number.

I didn't expect to hear from them. Months passed, and as I had anticipated, I heard nothing. Then one late summer day when I returned home, there was a note from Robert to me about Harper and Row. They wanted to publish the book. I let them and it became a best-seller.

In addition, imagining Jesus in my prayer has helped with the inner healing of my soul. Growing up and in my early adulthood, I was often subjected to belittling comments and shaming words. Soon I began to take other people's opinions of me as my own self-image. The biting remarks I had heard from other people, I now told myself. Anxiety and depression resulted.

In 1992 my disability was diagnosed. I received thorough neurological testing for brain damage. After analyzing the testing, the researchers said they didn't know how I finished high school, much less have written books for publishers like Paulist and Harper/Collins. I knew how—through the touch of Jesus on my heart.

After my diagnosis, I continued to let my imagination be a doorway by which Jesus could heal me. Each night I let my mind return to one or more scenes when I was deeply embarrassed or disparaged because of my disability. Early on I returned to the scene when, in junior high, a teacher told me, "You are no good at all." I would be in the scene, but this time Jesus would be in it with me. The bright light of his presence surrounded me. I heard him say, "You are a wonderful, good, though misunderstood, child. You are precious to me. You can discount all that the teacher tells you. You are precious in my sight." After many months of going back to such scenes with Jesus and hearing his affirming words, my anxiety lessened. I rejoiced in the goodness Jesus had built in to me. Rather than pour scorn on myself as others had, I began to see myself as Jesus saw me. My healing is still ongoing and much in me needs to healed, but I am assured the one true healer of souls walks beside me.

Imaginative prayer has helped me draw closer to God. Often I imagine Jesus sitting beside me, his hand entwined in mine. I just sit there enjoying the closeness, looking into his eyes and receiving an eternity of love through those same eyes. At times I am able to return some of that love to him that first filled me.

Practical Steps

▶ The first step in imaginative prayer is to ask the Holy Spirit to guide your prayer time. Give the amount of time you spend over to him. Let yourself still down; gently whisper over and over again a short prayer that calls upon Jesus, such as "Jesus, Lord Jesus."

▶ Go further into the deep relaxation of God.

▶ Take time to prayerfully relax. Begin with picturing Jesus. This is not hard work. The point is to let the Spirit guide you. You might take a picture of Jesus from your wall or from a book and simply look at it. Now close your eyes and picture that face. At times all of us have fuzzy imaginations. Just having a vague sense of Jesus being near you is enough.

▶ From here, imagine him placing his hand on your shoulder or taking your hand. Let the feelings of warmth, closeness, and unconditional love flow over you. Rest in that scene. Sometimes images can trigger quiet, imageless moments of resting in God's love, contemplative moments. If this happens to you, relax in the contemplative stillness as long as you want before moving on.

Scripture Reflection

We come to God for more than healing; we come to become one with him, to have our hearts beat in sync with his heart. One way of doing this is to put yourself in a scene from Scripture. This is a form of prayer particularly recommended by Saint Ignatius Loyola. First, slowly read the passage you have chosen. Now close your eyes, and as vividly as you can, envision the scene; try to experience the smells, the sights, the feel of the wind. Place yourself in the scene. For instance, if you pick the scene of the Annunciation from Luke 1:26–38, see the angel; see the Virgin; feel the light of heaven flow down on you as it flows on Mary. Let the totality of your being be caught up in the scene.

If you don't know what to choose, ask the Spirit to guide you to different scenes. I vividly remember seeing, when I was four or five, the picture of Jacob's dream of angels ascending and descending a staircase into heaven, as recounted in Genesis 28:10–22. It so affected me that when I pictured that scene, I saw myself in it, immersed in the wonder of it all. Again, such imaginative moments may lead you into a deep, contemplative resting in God. Remain in that restful state as long as seems good to you.

Another way of using this type of prayer is to picture a time in your life when you were deeply hurt. Imagine the scene as if you were there. Now imagine Jesus in that scene, his light filling the room. His presence takes away much of the sting of the hurt. Now imagine Jesus speaking words of reassurance to you, telling you that whatever it is that happened to you, his love is stronger, that he believes in you, finds you beautiful and good. Think of the negative messages others may have said to you, and then think of words Jesus might say to counter those messages. In my case, in a scene when someone called me lazy or slothful, Jesus would say, "You are my child, I love you. The person saying these words about you just does not understand that you are doing the best you can. When I look on you, I see you as beautiful."

Messages like this from Jesus counter the negative messages we may have received from others. We begin to stop saying lies about ourselves to ourselves and begin to access the deeper levels of truth that result from preparing our souls for intimate meeting with God. Imaginative prayer can also usher us into the joys of loving God for God's own sake. Picture such scenes as the scene of the Lord appearing in the temple to Isaiah, the Transfiguration, the New Jerusalem descending from Heaven and many other scenes. Put yourself in those scenes and behold the majesty of God. Thank him for his beauty and majesty. Stand in awe of the one who is so other than us and yet becomes so tenderly close to us.

Another way to lose yourself in the mystery of God is to remember vividly a time when God has touched you. Relive those scenes, and the presence of God will become real in the present moment. As Ignatius Loyola said in his exercises, "imagine...and taste the infinite savor of the sweetness of Divinity."

Guided Meditation

Allow yourself to grow still. See yourself surrounded by God's holy and healing light. Feel the light touch and warm your skin. Breathe in the light.

Each time you inhale, breathe in the light until you are soaked in a warming, healing radiance inside and out. Each time you exhale, breathe out negativity and fear.

Feel the light ease and relax the muscles of your neck and shoulder. The healing light moves to your arms. Your arms become heavy and relaxed with the healing light of God. The healing warmth moves into the muscles of your back, your chest, your stomach, permeating you with the love of God. Your legs and feet are warmed and relaxed by the light of God. Rest for a few minutes in the relaxing stillness.

Put yourself in the scene of the Transfiguration. See Jesus, accompanied by Moses and Elijah, shine with the blazing light of heaven. Stay with this scene a while.

Put yourself in the scene of Jacob's dream, seeing angels traverse up and down the ladder to heaven. Let the dazzling brightness of heaven pour down on you, catching you up, for a moment, in the glory.

Take time to rest in the stillness for as long as seems good to you.

CHAPTER 10

The Mystical Gift of Tears

The "gift of tears" is referred to often in historic Catholic, Orthodox, and Protestant sources on mysticism. Alan Jones, an expert on the early mystics of the desert, sums it up this way:

> The "gift of tears"…is concerned with something much more radical, threatening and life-bearing than the occasional and necessary release from tension that "having a good cry" affords. The tears of which the desert bears witness are not tears of rage, self-pity, or frustration. They are a gift, and their fruit is always joy."[79]

---

79. Alan W. Jones, *Soul Making: The Desert Way of Spirituality* (San Francisco: HarperOne, 1989), 82.

❧ JIM'S STORY

Several years back I met a man named Jim who told me how Christ had touched his heart. He had graduated with an MBA and become a stockbroker in Southern California, his mind fixed on becoming wealthy. At that time, he told me, he had a bumper sticker on his car that proclaimed, "He who dies with the most toys wins."

A handsome athlete who jogged eight miles a day, Jim had no problem finding dates, but he had encountered great problems in finding an enduring relationship. One young woman he had dated briefly was deeply into cocaine. He accompanied her to a party where she later overdosed. She went into convulsions and became unresponsive right before his eyes because of a buildup of cocaine in her system.

After she was pronounced dead at the emergency room, Jim went numb. Though he had no particular attachment to the dead young woman, her death shook him to the core. It was as if his heart was a tightly wound ball of confusion. He fled from the emergency room and found the hospital chapel, sinking into a pew. Remembering the church of his childhood years, he felt safe. His eyes locked in on a beautiful Byzantine icon of Christ the Teacher. Christ was holding the Gospels in his hands; his face looked alive. The figure's eyes seemed to be focused on Jim; Jesus' eyes looked down on him with infinite love and tenderness.

Tears began to course down Jim's face—tears of repentance for the aimlessness of his life. A deep calm settled inside him. Just looking at that icon seemed like coming home. It was as though Christ's presence was in the whole chapel, which felt timeless, beneficent and calm. Jim felt loved and nourished inside and out.

In the midst of such love, he saw clearly the shallowness of his life. He prayed, "I have been so far from you, O Jesus, so very far." It was as though he could hear Christ whispering to him in response, "And all the while I have been so very near you, waiting. I will always be near you."

Jim let those mystical moments become a living symbol around which he began to organize his life. He started attending church again and began developing Christian friends, reading spiritual books and praying. Tears played a key role in his transformation. At times he cried tears of contrition. The confusion of his life began to empty out of him through tears. Tears welled up in his eyes at the thought of the tenderness of God's mercy and the unsurpassable beauty of his presence.

The tears washed away his neurotic, perfectionist self, calling forth his genuine identity, the self that God created in him. The tears knitted his soul to Christ, helping form an enduring relationship with his Savior. The tears lightened his heart, leaving him with a heavenly joy.

Eventually he left his job as a stockbroker and returned to school to earn a graduate degree in religious education, becoming a religious education coordinator for a large parish.

New life burst into Jim through his tears. They had a powerful cathartic effect. He had been gifted with what many major traditions of Christianity call "the gift of tears."

Tears come as we learn to live from the depths of our being. They come when we hit rock bottom and become keenly aware of our hurt, our fragility, and our helplessness before God. They cleanse the soul through what the Eastern Churches call a "joy-making sorrow."

One way of keeping that "joy-making sorrow" alive in the East was *penthos*, called compunction in the West. *Penthos* means a piercing of the heart manifested in tears. We tend to pretend and put on a false self when we are stressed or hurting. *Penthos* breaks away that false self. As Jones puts it, "The tears are like the breaking of waters of the womb before the birth of a child."[80]

---

80. Ibid., 85.

The Protestant mystic and evangelical preacher Frederic Brotherton Meyer said:

Tears relieve the burning brain, as a shower the electric clouds. Tears discharge the insupportable agony of the heart, as an overflow lessens the pressure of the flood against the dam. Tears are the material out of which heaven weaves its brightest rainbows. Tears are transmuted into the jewels of better life, as the wounds in the oyster turn to pearls.[81]

In the Roman West, Saint Francis of Assisi taught "that those who strive after the perfect life should cleanse themselves daily with streams of tears." Bonaventure, his biographer, expressed it this way, "Although he had already attained extraordinary purity of heart and body, he did not cease to cleanse the eyes of his soul with a continuous flood of tears…"[82]

Aelred of Rievaulx, the great Scottish Cistercian of the twelfth century, hardly ever prayed without tears. When he talked with God, "he bathed his whole face with a fountain of tears." Aelred called tears signs of perfect prayer, "the embassies between God and man."[83]

For John Climacus, a seventh-century monk, tears were something more than an inward movement of grace. They formed part of the spiritualization of the body and of the physical senses. Spiritual mourning for him "leads to spiritual laughter; it is a wedding garment, not a funeral robe…."[84] In a beautiful passage he writes, "Joy goes with sorrow like honey in a comb: As I ponder the true nature of compunction, I find myself amazed by the way in which inward

81. Frederick Meyer, *Abraham or the Obedience of Faith* (New York: Fleming H. Revell Company, 1890), 184.

82. Bonaventure, *The Life of Saint Francis*, trans., Ewert H. Cousins (San Francisco: HarperOne, 2005), 50.

83. Walter Daniel, ed. Maurice Powicke. *The Life of Aelred of Rievaulx* (London: Nelson, 1963), 20.

84. John Climacus, *John Climacus: The Ladder of Divine Ascent*, trans. Colm Luibheid and Norman Russell (New York, Paulist Press, 1982), 24.

joy and gladness mingle with what we call mourning and grief, like honey in a comb."[85]

Some people's temperament meant that they could not weep easily. John understood this and wrote that for those people, the simple helplessness of their heart before God substituted for tears. Ignatius Loyola possessed the "gift of tears," and ordinarily he wept six or seven times a day. A fellow Jesuit was troubled he did not yet possess the "gift of tears." Ignatius ordered a letter be written to him on Ignatius' behalf. The letter, full of common sense, said that since this particular Jesuit was full of "compassion for the miseries of your neighbors and want to help them and do all in your power to carry out your desire, no other tears and no other tenderness of heart are necessary....So do not be troubled by the lack of external tears...."[86]

There have been times in my life when tears of compunction emptied my soul. These tears were a blessing, a gift. After the diagnosis of my disability, it was time to let go of all the anger I had built up inside of me for those who had not shown compassion to me because of my undiagnosed disability. They were not at fault. I did not even know the cause; how could they? Even if they were at fault, I needed to forgive. I also needed to feel sorrow and turn back from resentments I held on to.

I remember the tears trickling down my face, cleansing my body and my soul. Since I do not weep easily, it had to be God's gift.

Although tears come slowly for me, I simply pray that God send me tender compassion of heart in their place. I have to trust John Climacus and Ignatius Loyola that the gift of external tears is not for everyone at all times and to pray for the interior disposition of compassion instead.

I remember the death of my mother at age 93 in 2007. She was in assisted living for Alzheimer's patients. Till the very end she knew

---

85. Ibid., 24

86. Paul Van Dyke, *Ignatius Loyola, The Founder of the Jesuits* (New York: C. Scribner's Sons, 1926), 316.

me, and the sweetness and joy in her personality remained despite the dementia. I had been out West conducting retreats and was scheduled to fly to Boston to give a parish retreat. The plane from Dallas to Boston had to turn back halfway to Boston because of a blizzard in New England. I was exhausted. After I landed back in Dallas, the phone beeped with a call from my cousin Jane. After a normal breakfast, Mother had turned unresponsive, and the nurse thought she might die in a few hours. A heavy weight bore down on me. I felt as though I were sinking through the floor, but liberating tears would not flow. I desperately wanted to get a plane home in time to see her, but the next plane out was not until morning. My emotions manifested themselves in a sharp, unbearably painful headache. I did not sleep at all that night, and tears still would not come. At five in the morning, the call came that Mother had died. I arrived home that afternoon.

My cousins Jane and Betty went with me into the viewing room to see my mother. Both had their arms around me, and with their support and prayers, the tears began to flow, as I sobbed and mourned a dear and wonderful woman who had had such a positive role in my life. Those tears were indeed an unexpected gift from a gracious God who knew my grief needed to flow outward through tears.

Practical Steps

▶ Take time and journal on the gift of tears.

▶ Have there ever been times in your life when tears gave way to joy? Write a few sentences describing that time.

▶ Have there been times in your life when tears effected a reconciliation, hearts coming together after a time of misunderstanding? Write about that for a while.

▶ Do you easily feel sorrow when you have failed God or others, experiencing the heart-soothing tears of compunction? If not, take time and pray daily for a softening of your heart at the inconceivable mercy of God.

▶ Take time in your prayer periods to develop a heart full of compassion. In your prayer imagine people who are hurting, victims of injustice. In your mind's eye look at their faces. What do you see? What do you think they are feeling? Ask God for the gift of tears to carve out a space in your heart for compassion.

▶ In older monastic manuals and in the Eastern Liturgy, there are many prayers for the gift of tears. Pray often for the cleansing stream that is the gift of tears.

▶ In your church setting, let it be known that tears are OK. Often when people are deeply moved at church or in church groups, they don't understand why the tears come, and they feel embarrassed and awkward. Make sure they understand such tears as a gift, by giving the biblical and historical use of tears in prayer. Remind them that tears in a group can pass on the tenderness of God's nearness one to another.

Scripture Reflection

The shortest verse in Scripture is "Jesus wept" (John 11:35). He mourned the death of his close friend Lazarus.

For the woman who bathed Jesus' feet with her tears and dried them with her hair, tears expressed deep, tender devotion (Luke 7:38).

For Saint Paul, tears expressed great love and earnestness of heart. He tells the Corinthians, "I wrote you out of much distress and anguish of heart and with many tears...to let you know the abundant love I have for you" (2 Corinthians 2:4). In his letter to the Romans, he suggests that tears are a way of feeling empathy with others: "Rejoice with those who rejoice, weep with those who weep" (Romans 12:15).

Tears can also be joy-making. The Psalmist exclaimed, "For his anger is but for a moment; his favour is for a lifetime. Weeping may linger for the night, but joy comes with the morning" (Psalm 30:5). In addition, "May those who sow in tears reap with shouts of joy" (Psalm 126:5).

Guided Meditation

Let your heart grow still. Let the peace of an everlasting love take hold in your soul as your limbs relax, your torso relaxes, and your soul is flooded by God's calm.

Imagine you are in a different place, a different time: the Holy Land during the time of Christ. See the woman who tenderly washes Jesus' feet with her tears. Pray for a gift of devotion and adoration equal to that woman's.

Pray the following prayer:

> Lord, soften my heart. Fill me inwardly with tenderness in response to your great mercy. And if it is right for me, if it is time for me, help me to express that tenderness in tears. Strengthen my heart through helping me develop a great devotion to the humanity of your love. Help me weep with compassion with those in need, a compassion that sets my feet on the road to actually helping and soothing others' hurt. Amen.

CHAPTER 11

Becoming Channels of God's Healing

We are called to be instruments of God's healing and peace. When we open up our inward parts for God to transform us, our touch, our manner, the quality of our speech, our presence can convey his love to others. Throughout my reading of the lives of mystics, I have found over and over again stories of individuals who went on a journey into God's love, a journey in which they faced, with God's help, their inner demons, then went out to love others with the same quality of love with which they had been loved.

Francis healed by his very presence. Just being around Bernard of Clairvaux made people want to start a whole new life. The charismatic elders in the Eastern Church, beginning with Anthony of the Desert, were people who spent great periods in the solitude of prayer, and out of that prayer, especially in the latter part of their lives, became healers of body and soul and compassionate readers of hearts.

✤ MARGARET'S STORY

When I was fourteen, I encountered a Baptist mystic, Margaret Cox, a lover of God like Saint Francis, who turned my life around. Before I met her, my life had become bitter. My last year in junior high had been near catastrophic. I had failed two courses, and only summer school kept me from repeating a grade. Life at home also became difficult. My dad, normally a wonderful father, suffered through a period of diagnosed mental illness, and he could be terrifying at times. Both home and school left me numb with fear.

My as yet undiagnosed right hemisphere brain damage affected nearly all my daily activities, making dressing and grooming, and organizing paper and books, confusing. It impaired my ability to concentrate. However, the left side of my brain, the part that handles words and concepts, worked well. My ability to comprehend words and use them reached a near college level. My family, my teachers, and my peers didn't understand. Many saw me as a lazy, careless, and messy underachiever. I blamed myself more than any of my critics and felt helpless to change.

By the time I met Margaret Cox, I was near dead inside.

She wore several hats at my high school, teaching creative writing as well as serving as guidance counselor. Early in my first year, one of my teachers passed on to her an essay I had written about my favorite poet, T.S. Eliot, and his spiritual poetry. Miss Cox saw through the nearly illegible handwriting and messy sheets to the content of what I had written and loved what she read. She called me into her office. "What I read shows promise, lots of promise. I want you to join the creative writing class I teach. And by the way, you are the first student at this school I know of who reads T.S. Eliot. He's also my favorite poet."

I joined her class and from then on I received a lot of attention from Miss Cox. A published poet herself, she spent hours preparing me for writing contests and oratorical contests, many of which I won. My grades turned from D's and F's to A's and B's, especially after she passed on the message to my teachers to grade me on the content of my work and ignore the bad handwriting and messiness of my papers.

But it was more than her encouragement that turned my life around. She conveyed more with her presence than with her words. Depth, love, and God filled her personality. In my early days around her, we did not talk about God, but it was obvious the love of God pervaded her. Just being near her I felt ushered into God's own presence. I had no doubt she loved me. But the love that came from her came from more than just her; it also came from God, because, as I later found out, her life was soaked in the beauty of God's caring.

Then the day came when we began to talk about spirituality. She knew from how fond I was of Eliot's spiritual poetry that I also was on a spiritual journey, and that freed her, over a period of several weeks, to tell me about her own spiritual life. A devout Baptist, she read widely in spiritual literature, including Protestants like Catherine Marshall and Catholics like G.K. Chesterton. She loved Chesterton's *Saint Francis of Assisi*. As a teenager, she experienced the tender light of God's love after nearly drowning in a stream. "I felt God all around me and all through me," she told me. "I knew from then on that my life's task was to spread his love."

After that, she studied the Bible, reading it slowly, meditating on the words, daily opening up to God. She told me she now felt God's presence in the core of her being, a presence that never seemed to leave her.

She not only affected my life, but the lives of hundreds of students through the years. I dedicated my first book, *Sounds of Wonder*, to her.

Miss Cox is an example of someone who has been profoundly touched by God and who went out and touched others with that same sacred presence. She was a healer, an inspirer, God's very hands and feet.

Mystics who heal have been part of Christian tradition from the very beginning. In Russia, particularly in the nineteenth century and early twentieth century, monastic elders emerged, and thousands of people would flock to see them. The word they used for this type of soul-healing elders was *startsy*.

One that stands out is Saint Seraphim of Sarov. He taught the mystical life to laypersons. Thousands visited him in his hermitage at the monastery in Sarov. Seraphim was canonized by the Russian Orthodox Church in 1903. Pope John Paul II referred to him as a saint in his book *Crossing the Threshold of Hope*.

It seems from the beginning of his monastic career, Seraphim's winsome personality calmed people who came in contact with him. His real ministry to the world began after decades of solitude, enduring human temptations. With God's help, through countless hours of prayer, he faced down the gloom in the world and those elements within himself that would distract him from his course. He had many beautiful spiritual visions in that process.

In his later years, people lined up every day to see him. He embraced them warmly, calling them each "My joy" or exuberantly saying, "Christ is risen." At times he could read hearts, knowing people's circumstances, difficulties at work and even sins, before they came to him. Moreover, with deep tenderness he would give them advice. Suffering people from all over Russia found their way to him, bringing domestic problems, problems of the spirit and problems in their work. He believed rich, warming inner prayer was for all Christians, not just monastics. Such closeness to God included both God and neighbor.

Nicholas Motovilov, a close friend of Seraphim's, gives a personal description of how just being near the saint brought one into the presence of God. Seraphim had been talking with him about how Christians should acquire the fullness of the Holy Spirit.

"My need," Motovilov responded, "is to understand this well!"

Then Seraphim took him firmly by the shoulders and told him, "We are both together, son, in the Spirit of God! Why aren't you looking at me?"

Motovilov replied, "I cannot look, Father, because…Your face is brighter than the sun, and my eyes ache in pain!"

Father Seraphim said, "Fear not, my son; you too have become as bright as I. You too are now in the fullness of God's Spirit…"

Bending his head toward Motovilov, Seraphim whispered softly in his ear. "See, the grace of God has come to comfort your contrite heart, as a loving mother…Come, son, why do you not look me in the eyes? Just look and fear not! The Lord is with us!"

Then Motovilov looked at his face and saw a "blinding light spreading several yards around and throwing a sparkling radiance across the snow blanket on the glade and into the snowflakes which besprinkled the great elder and me. Can one imagine," he said, "the state in which I then found myself?"

"How do you feel now?" Father Seraphim asked.

"Unwontedly well!" Motovilov replied.

"But well in what way? How in particular?" Seraphim asked.

He answered, "I feel a calmness and peace in my soul that I cannot express in words!"

Seraphim said, "See now with what joy the Lord consoles you while yet here! What else do you feel, my son?"

He answered, "An unwonted warmth!"

Seraphim asked him how he could feel a warmth since snow and ice covered everything.

Motovilov answered, "Such as there is in the bath-house, when they pour the water on the stone and the steam rises in a cloud."

Seraphim explained further, "Of course this warmth is not in the air but in us. It is that very warmth about which the Holy Spirit in the words of the prayer makes us cry out to the Lord: 'Warm me with the warmth of Thy Holy Spirit!'"[87] A man and his wife visited Seraphim. Both were indifferent toward God and faith. Their meeting with Seraphim changed that attitude. Seraphim gave them a talk about the reality of God and the comfort of God's consolation. As he talked, something profound happened in the deep hearts of the couple. The husband writes of that encounter:

> This talk did not take more than an hour. But such an hour! I never had anything like this in my whole life. Throughout the talk I felt in my heart an inexplicable heavenly sweetness which came from God knows where, and which could not be compared with anything on earth. Even till now I cannot recall it without tears...and a most vivid sense of joy in all my being.[88]

Most of us can't spend years in solitude and prayer, like Seraphim, to prepare us to become channels of God's healing, but we can take time each week for God's brightness to fill us. When we bathe in the radiance of his splendor, we too become radiant with his presence.

In many ways, the active life and the contemplative life are one. Christ was a contemplative, a mystic. He spent long nights absorbing the love of God in prayer before his activity the next day. In him is a beautiful blend of mystic and active doer. Both the active and contemplative were one for him. His healing, his teaching, and his redeeming activity came out of a profound union with the Father. And so it should be for us. We cannot separate the active life from the contemplative life; they are one.

Our soaking up God's love enables us to go out into the world and concretely touch others with the same love with which he has

---

87. Adapted from G.P. Fedotov, ed., *A Treasury of Russian Spirituality* (New York: Sheed and Ward, 1948), 266–79.

88. Archimandrite Lazarus Moore, *An Extraordinary Peace: St. Seraphim, Flame of Sarov* (Port Townsend, WA: Anaphora Press, 2009), 148.

touched us. As we travel along our journey into God's love, we need to wash our brothers' and sisters' feet, reaching out like Christ to comfort, feed, and help those in need.

In us, Maclaren points out, is on one side what he calls "the contemplative life of interior union with God…the other is practical obedience in the work God has called us to." He continues, "These two are both capable of being raised to their highest power, and of being discharged with the most unrestricted and joyous activity, on condition of our keeping close to Christ." [89] He further notes, "The weary schism between the active and the contemplative life is closed up. Mary and Martha end their long variance, and gazing on his face does not hinder active obedience, nor does doing him service distract from beholding his beauty."[90]

Evelyn Underhill states that "true mysticism is active and practical, not passive and theoretical. It is an organic life process, a something which the whole self does; not something as to which its intellect holds an opinion."[91]

Mysticism softens our hearts, giving us great empathy with those who suffer, helping us reach out in compassion. Isaac of Nineveh, who lived in the seventh century, suggests, "Let the weight of compassion in you weigh you down until you feel in your heart the same compassion that God feels for the world."[92]

Closeness to God not only impels us to care for the poor, the lonely, and the rejected, but to partner with him in the transformation of society. When God calls near to him, he also calls us to work for justice and peace and the rights of those not yet born. Many mystics in the history of Christianity worked for significant changes in

89. Alexander Maclaren, *Expositions of Holy Scripture: The Gospel according to St. John, IX to XIV* (New York: A.C. Armstrong and Sons, 1908), 29.

90. Alexander Maclaren, *The Epistles of John, Jude and the Book of Revelation* (New York: Hodder and Stoughton, 1910), 368.

91. Evelyn Underhill, as quoted in Susan Rakoczy, *Great Mystics and Social Justice: Walking on the Two Feet of Love* (New York: Paulist Press, 2006), 11.

92. Rakoczy, 15.

the world around them. This service can be joyful, as Maclaren reminds us: "Self-sacrifice at the bidding of Jesus Christ is the recipe for the highest, the most exquisite, the most godlike gladnesses of which the human heart is capable."[93]

Susan Rakoczy, in her wonderful book *Great Mystics and Social Justice*, writes, "True ministry, whether in the fourteenth century or today, flows from intimacy with God, while this intimacy continually pushes us into the heart of the world."[94]

One mystic, Saint Catherine of Siena, whom Rakoczy described as a "social mystic," knew the heights of intimacy with God even as she partnered with God to transform the society of her time. Part of Catherine's mission was hands-on care of the poor, nursing those sick with plague, feeding the hungry. Catherine, in her *Dialogue with God*, presents God as saying to her, "The poor are the hands which will open the gates of eternal life to you if you give alms with wholehearted love."[95]

She wrote letters to political and Church leaders, urging them to let God's peace prevail rather that the evil of the feuds and wars that ravaged Italy during the fourteenth century. She upbraided, often effectively, the leadership of her time for neglecting the poor. A simple young woman of prayer, she influenced bishops, the Pope, and the rulers of her time. She spent three years in solitude and prayer, soaking in God's love, experiencing the height of ecstasy. After those three years, she reached out to the world. She denounced the evils and scandals of the Church and worked for radical reform.

Rakoczy documents the work for justice in this very real world by many of the great mystics of the Church. Work for change in society is rootless unless rooted in the depths of God. We are called, she suggests, not only to care for the poor and helpless personally but to a "political love" that changes unmerciful structures of society

93. Maclaren, *John Vol. 3*, 28.

94. Rakoczy, 29.

95. Ibid., 217.

into merciful structures. She quotes Edward Schillebeeckx when she writes, "Without prayer or mysticism politics soon becomes cruel and barbaric; without political love, prayer or mysticism becomes sentimental...."[96] Indeed, God calls us to partner with him in the transforming and healing of creation.

God's love not only affects us, but affects all creation, the whole universe. My grandfather "Pop" was half North Carolina Cherokee, a baptized Baptist, but in touch with Native American sensibilities, and with a heart in tune with creation. His and my grandmother's little cottage was situated on a bluff high above the Chattahoochee. Rocks, rapids, and the bright greenery of the shore below his house presented a startling scene of beauty.

When I was little, I saw him spend long periods standing on the bluff looking down at the scene, the ground and vegetation near him, and the horizon high above the opposite bluff.

One day when he was surveying the world around him, I asked him, "Pop, what are you doing?"

He replied with his Appalachian accent, "I'm looking at what's in front of me."

"Why do you look so long?" I probed further.

"Because," he said, "if you look long enough, it will all shimmer and you will see the glory."

Pop, in his simplicity, realized deep down in his heart what is hard for us more sophisticated moderns to realize: that we are tied together heart and soul with the whole of the universe.

British Baptist evangelical and mystic, Frederick Brotherton Meyer, a close friend of the evangelist Dwight L. Moody, realized this vision of interconnectedness with all creation as only a contemplative can. In his devotional commentary on the book of Hebrews, he writes:

---

96. Ibid., 204.

...amid all natural variety, there is a marvelous unity. Every part of the universe interlocks by subtle and delicate links with every other part. You cannot disturb the balance anywhere without sending a shock of disturbance through the whole system. And all this because, if you penetrate to Nature's heart, you meet God. [97]

He then goes on to say, "Creation is the vesture of Christ. He wraps himself about in its ample folds."[98]

The Catholic mystic Saint Francis had a special relationship with creation; he preached with great fervor to the birds. They gazed at him attentively and would not leave until Francis made the sign of the cross over them. Then they all left together. Bonaventure, in his life of Francis, writes, "When he considered the primordial source of all things, he was filled with even more abundant piety, calling creatures, no matter how small, by the name of brother or sister, because he knew they had the same source as himself." [99]

Bonaventure, who himself walked in the steps of Francis, later said, "Taking perceptible things as a mirror, we see God *through* them—through his traces, so to speak; but we also see him *in* them...we are led to contemplate God *in* all the creatures that enter our mind through the bodily senses."[100]

Jonathan Edwards, the great Puritan mystic, often took long, solitary, prayerful walks in the woods, during which he meditated, seeing God's reflection in creation. He wrote that God "seemed to appear in everything; in the sun, moon, and stars; in the clouds, and blue sky; in the grass, flowers and trees; in the water, and all

---

97. F.B. Meyer, *The Way into the Holiest; Expositions of the Epistle to the Hebrews* (New York: F.H. Revell, 1893).

98. Meyer.

99. Bonaventure, as quoted in Cousins, 23.

100. José De Vinck, *The Works of Bonaventure: Cardinal, Seraphic Doctor, and Saint, Vol. 1: Mystical Opuscula* (Paterson, NJ: St. Anthony Guild Press, 1960), 18.

nature."[101] Eastern Church father Isaac of Nineveh says that the experience of God opens us up to our connection with all creatures: "The heart that is inflamed in this way embraces the entire creation—man, birds, animals At the recollection of them, and at the sight of them, such a man's eyes fill with tears that arise from the great compassion which presses on his heart." [102]

We do not grow close to God alone. We do not taste the sweetness of his presence alone. We are not strengthened by his touch alone. We always encounter God connected with our brothers and sisters and the whole of creation. Closeness to God commissions us to be channels of God's healing for our fellow humans and all creation. When we fail to accept this commission, our words about God can become saccharin and shallow.

People today yearn for sacred presence. We cannot will our personalities to carry that presence. There are no "five easy steps" to reflecting God's love. We can only soak ourselves in his presence and let him infiltrate the whole of our personalities

Practical Steps

In a congregation, helping people develop skills for prayerful reflection and encouraging private prayer and group contemplative prayer can change the whole atmosphere of the Church. Newcomers can feel God just by stepping into a church filled with prayerful people. The tenor of worship takes on a depth and beauty heretofore not known.

Few of us have the time to pray as much as Saint Seraphim, Saint Francis, or Saint Teresa of Avila, but we can still carve out time in our day for God. In our prayer we can include our wounded world and let our prayer impel us to go out and become a bridge to God

---

101. Jonathan Edwards, as quoted in Fanning, 18.

102. Isaac of Nineveh, as quoted in K.M. George, *The Silent Roots: Orthodox Perspectives on Christian Spirituality* (Geneva: World Council of Churches Publications, 1994), 62–65.

for the dispossessed and rejected. In our small ways, each day we can become a bit like Seraphim, spreading God by our presence, radiating calm.

Journal on ways you can do concrete activities to help encourage contemplative prayer in your church. Think about ways you can spread the compassion of Christ to others.

Remember a time when you experienced God's healing touch from the presence of another person. Write about how that felt and how you can extend that same healing to others.

Scripture Reflection

God showers his caring love upon the sparrows and the lilies (Matthew 6:26–30). The Scriptures point to creation and all of nature as God's gracious gift. We should avoid injuring and exploiting or degrading that gift.

God's becoming incarnate in Jesus is full of saving significance for creation. "For the creation waits with eager longing for the revealing of the children of God," Paul writes in Romans 8:19.

We, like every other creature in creation, are made from the earth (Genesis 2:7, 9, 19). Scripture speaks of our kinship with other creatures in passages like Job 38—39 and Psalm 104.

God cares faithfully for us, and together we join in singing the "hymn of all creation" as expressed in Psalm 148. Redemption includes all creation (Ephesians 1:10).

God has placed us in a web of life that ties us together with our fellow humans and all creation. He calls us to be good stewards of creation. When we draw close to God, we draw close to this world God has made. God calls for us to care for his creation in the same way he does. We can become channels of his healing, revivifying love for all created things.

Guided Meditation

Let God's stillness flow through you, settling you down, calming you. Notice your breathing in and out. When you breathe in, breathe in God's love. When you breathe out, breathe out tension and anxiety.

Simply repeat the name Jesus, and let this healing name take you deeper and deeper into prayer, deeper and deeper into God.

In your memory, vividly recall some times when others by their very presence ushered you into God's presence. Recall their words, the look in their eyes, their whole manner. Say a prayer of thanks for having such people in your life's history.

Imagine that you are standing in a huge field of green grass. Beside you stands Jesus. In front of you are countless people who have been hurt, not only hurt personally, but neglected by society and even sometimes the Church. The poor, the ill, the lonely and left alone, those marginalized by our society based on consumption, all those denied their basic human dignity. Look at their faces; notice their eyes. What do some of the facial expressions say?

Fix your eyes on Jesus as he gazes over the crowd. See the tears of compassion stream down his face. He opens wide his arms, as though to embrace the whole crowd. Light streams from his heart, pouring over the whole throng, bringing healing, peace, love to each person.

Jesus now asks you to join him. He asks you to also stretch out your arms toward the people. You sense the light of God's presence that abides in your heart flowing out toward the crowd.

Remain there in stillness a few minutes.

Buried Treasure

Mysticism within the Protestant Tradition

One of the nearly untold stories of Christianity is that of mysticism in the Protestant tradition. Twenty years ago I discovered a devotional commentary on the Gospel of John, by Alexander Maclaren, a nineteenth-century, world-famous Baptist leader and early evangelical. For the encounter with God, Maclaren used heart language whose cadence and rhythm warmed and stilled my soul. His words sounded like those of medieval Catholic mystics like Bernard of Clairvaux. *This man is a mystic*, I said to myself. I read further in the commentary and found out, according to his own words, that he was very influenced by Saint Bernard as well as other mystics. I then saved my pennies and ordered all thirty-six large volumes of his commentaries on Scripture.

I found in his work a rich source of ideas for my sermons and for the books I wrote. Later, when most of his works were put online by Google Books, I searched for Maclaren's use of the word "mysticism" and variants and got 800 hits. The words "contemplative" and "contemplation" received 600 hits. In addition, "meditation" and related words turned up 839 hits.

Many scholars, especially rationalist Protestant scholars of the early twentieth century, had declared that mysticism was absent from the Reformation churches from the beginning. Yet here, 350 years after the Reformation, a prominent Baptist minister extolled mysticism as an almost necessary part of the Christian life.

Soon after studying Maclaren, I found another famous British Baptist minister, Frederick Brotherton Meyer, who ministered in the late nineteenth and early twentieth centuries. His writings were highly mystical, used Bernard of Clairvaux, and quoted the late medieval mystic Catherine of Siena at length. A close friend of Dwight L. Moody, he preached on both sides of the Atlantic, and his books reached hundreds of thousands.

In preparation for writing this current book, I researched further and found that Maclaren and Meyer were not just isolated oddities, but inheritors of a long mystical tradition that included the two major founders of Protestantism, Luther and Calvin. I uncovered source after source and found a tradition that could bring Catholics and Protestants closer, provide fresh new resources on mysticism and help open up the way for today's Protestants to rediscover mysticism within their own ranks. Catholics, too, can learn from these Protestant mystical writers. In the late nineteenth century, contemplative prayer and mysticism were kept within the confines of the Catholic monasteries and cloistered convents, not reaching the average Catholic in the pew. At that very same time, Protestants were teaching mysticism and contemplative prayer to whole congregations.

These Protestants can help us all grasp the simplicity, practicality, and warm human touch of mysticism and contemplative prayer.

In addition, they clearly center mysticism in its Biblical sources. As these Protestant mystics are rediscovered, Catholics may find themselves gobbling up their writings.

Within today's evangelical world, there is a flowering interest in contemplation, even Christian mysticism. Those who are interested in those topics are sometimes blamed for importing something Roman Catholic or the "New Age" movement. In actuality, as Protestants look deeper, they will find the mystical, contemplative tradition solidly, not only in Scripture but within their own faith traditions.

Luther and Calvin

The two major figures of the sixteenth-century reformation were Martin Luther and John Calvin. Both emphasized Scripture as the source of faith and life, but they also, in significant ways, preserved some of the heritage of the Church fathers and medieval mystics, especially Saint Bernard.

Luther scholar Reinhard Schwarz writes that "if we understand mysticism to be the inwardness of being united with God, then we find mysticism in Luther."[103] According to Bengt Hoffmann, mystical theology for Luther was the experience of God. "If we can define it that way Luther's spirituality had a significant mystical component."[104]

Over the last twenty years, scholars—especially on the Protestant side but also in some Catholic work—have found in their studies of Church history and systematic theology that the theology of the reformers "cannot be understood simply as the rediscovery of Holy Scripture or the return to the ancient Church, but that theologians like Martin Luther and John Calvin were also deeply rooted in me-

---

103. Reinhard Schwarz, "Martin Luther (1483–1546)," in *Grosse Mystiker. Leben und Wirken*, G. Ruhbach and J. Sudbrack, eds. (Munich, 1984), 185–202, 375–80.

104. Bengt R Hoffman, "Lutheran Spirituality," in *Spiritual Traditions for the Contemporary Church*, Robin Maas and Gabriel O'Donnell, eds., (Nashville: Abingdon Press, 1990), 150.

dieval theological traditions. In particular, this research has cast new light on their closeness to medieval mysticism."[105] This "closeness" had been strenuously denied at the beginning of the twentieth century by a "liberal" theology influenced by the Enlightenment and rationalism.

Johann Arndt and the German Pietists

An early seventeenth-century Lutheran minister, Johann Arndt, wrote books that spread deep, heart-felt mystical union with Christ to a large audience. Like Luther and Calvin, he was particularly inspired by Bernard of Clairvaux, Thomas à Kempis, and the Dominican mystic John Tauler as well as the medieval Franciscan mystic Angela de Foligno. Instead of the dry, scholarly, "scholastic" exactness that prevailed in the Lutheranism of his time, knowledge of God for Arndt "does not consist in words or in mere learning but in a living, loving, gracious, powerful consolation in which through grace one tastes the sweetness, joyousness, loveliness, and graciousness of God in his heart."[106]

Arndt also had a heart for the socially disadvantaged, and his writings spurred care for the underprivileged. He maintained an orthodox Lutheranism while borrowing heavily from medieval mystics. He wrote that our coming alive in Christ was "the end of all theology and the whole of Christianity. This is the union with God, the marriage with our heavenly Bridegroom, Jesus Christ, the... living faith, the new birth, Christ's dwelling in us."[107]

After Arndt came a powerful movement of heart knowledge of God by proponents of a movement called German Pietists. Phillip Jakob Spener, the founder of this movement, constantly referred

---

105. Dagmar Heller, "Union with Christ: John Calvin and the Mysticism of St. Bernard," *Ecumenical Review*, July 1996.

106. Fanning, 143.

107. Arndt, 7.

back to Arndt in his teaching,[108] and Arndt has been called the father of German Pietism.[109]

Pietism can be called a mystical movement. "Pietism was a source for much of John Wesley's spirituality and through him it touched North American nineteenth-century revivalism and the Evangelical movement of the twentieth century," states Peter Erb in his masterful study of Pietism.[110]

The Early Puritans

The early Puritans who first settled New England were, to some extent, spiritual descendants of John Calvin and thus were imbued with mysticism. According to Puritan historian Charles Hambrick-Stowe, "Puritans knew and used classic devotional works."[111] They read mystics such as Augustine, Bernard of Clairvaux, and Thomas à Kempis, whose *The Imitation of Christ* appeared in Protestant editions. Words and phrases from medieval mystical classics found their way into the sermons, and devotional manuals therefore reached into the layperson in the pew.[112]

Cotton Mather, a famous New England clergyman, wrote of his father's mystical experiences: "in his latter Years, [his father] did not Record so many of [his] Heavenly Afflations, because they grew so frequent with him. And…the Flights of a Soul rapt up into a more Intimate Conversation with Heaven, are such as cannot be exactly Remembered."[113]

---

108. (Wikipedia)

109. Fanning, 144.

110. Erb, 2.

111. Charles E. Hambrick-Stowe, *The Practice of Piety: Puritan Devotional Disciplines in Seventeenth-Century New England* (Chapel Hill, NC: University of North Carolina Press, 1982), 28.

112. Ibid., 28.

113. Ibid., 217.

Jonathan Edwards, the New England Calvinist and Congregational clergyman who ministered in the early half of the eighteenth century, was a spiritual descendant of the New England Puritans. He was, as scholar Stephen Fanning firmly asserts, a mystic. He shared a unique spiritual closeness with his wife, Susan. He talks about her mystical closeness to God during a time of personal crisis. He recorded her words, saying she stated that the presence of God "sweetly smiled upon me….In consequence of this, I felt a strong desire to be alone with God, to go to him, without having any one to interrupt the silent and soft communion." In the following days, she had a "delightful sense of the immediate presence and love of God." She continued, "[T]he presence of God was so near, that I seemed scarcely conscious of anything else…and Christ appeared to me…my mind was so deeply impressed with the love of Christ, and a sense of his immediate presence…with a continual view of God as *nearer*, and as *my God*."[114] She went on to say, "My soul remained in a kind of heavenly Elysium." She seemed to perceive "a glow of divine love come down from the heart of Christ in heaven, into my heart." She "had an idea of a shining way, or path of light, between heaven and my soul." She felt "entirely swallowed up in God."[115]

As a teenage student at Yale, Edwards had the following spiritual experience while reading 1 Timothy 1:27:

> There came into my soul, and was as it were diffused through it, a sense of the glory of the divine being;…I thought with myself…how happy I should be, if I might enjoy that God, and be wrapt up to God in heaven.[116]

---

114. Jonathan Edwards, *The Works of Jonathan Edwards, Vol. 1* (London, 1834; repr. Peabody, MA: Hendrickson Publishers, 1998), civ.

115. Ibid., cvii-cviii.

116. George S. Claghorn, ed., "Edwards, Personal Narrative," *The Works of Jonathan Edwards, Vol. 16, Letters and Personal Writings* (New Haven and London: Yale University Press, 1998), 793.

When Edwards was at his first pastorate in New York, he would take times for solitude in nature "for contemplation on divine things, and secret converse with God; and had many sweet hours there."[117]

John Wesley

John Wesley was a famous evangelist and founder of the Methodist movement. As we have already mentioned, Wesley was greatly influenced through his associations with the German Pietists. William Law, the famed British spiritual writer, was also another influence. Law read widely the mystical writers throughout the different eras of the Church, among them Cassian, Tauler, Cusa and Ruysbroeck. Wesley began his theological studies at Christ Church Oxford, where he began his studies of the Church fathers. He was also inspired through reading the mystics of the seventeenth century.[118] Fanning states that in Wesley's expanding ministry, "he taught concepts commonly found in mystical writings throughout the centuries..."[119] In the mid-eighteenth century Wesley gathered together and published fifty volumes he called "the Christian Library." The library consisted of extracts from the early Church fathers as well as Wesley's favorite mystics.[120] This library was used by Wesley's followers throughout his life and long after his death.

The notion that later in life Wesley suddenly repudiated mystical influences and abandoned them forever is an erroneous one. Wesley does have some negative things to say about Moravian mysticism, but as Wesley expert Frank Whaling assures us, he did not repudiate mysticism. "The fifty volumes of his Christian Library of 1750–1756 contained no works by Luther and Calvin but they did include the works of five French and three Spanish Roman Catholic mystics."[121]

---

117. Fanning, 193.

118. Ibid., 187.

119. Ibid., 187.

120. Ibid., 187.

121. Frank Whaling, ed., *John and Charles Wesley: Selected Prayers, Hymns, Journal Notes, Sermons, Letters and Treatises* (New York: Paulist Press, 1981), 10.

Wesley's doctrine of perfection was a toned-down version of the experience of the union with God found in the mystics. He, in turn, influenced the great revival movements of North America and the wing of the Wesleyan movement known as the Holiness Movement, and through them, the Holiness Pentecostal movement of our own time.

The founders of the Holiness Movement, which arose from the Wesleyans, used Wesley's Christian Library, and as Fanning puts it, "they acknowledged Tauler, John of the Cross and Ruusbroec as their spiritual ancestors." They advocated a "second blessing," an experience of Christian perfection, which was to them a mystical experience.[122]

Alexander Maclaren

Two late nineteenth-, early twentieth-century Baptist mystical writers stand out, Alexander Maclaren and Frederick Brotherton Meyer.

Alexander Maclaren, who received a classical education and won special awards in Biblical Hebrew and Biblical Greek, was a British Baptist minister who pastored a large church in Manchester, where he often preached sermons that included Christian mysticism, contemplation and meditation. He was twice president of the Baptist Union of Great Britain and named president of the World Baptist Congress in London in 1905. His heartfelt preaching drew thousands to his church in Manchester, and his *Expositions of Holy Scripture* have been loved and used by several generations of evangelicals.

Maclaren extolled the importance of Christian mysticism:

> Oh! brethren, do not be tempted, by any dread of mysticism, to deprive yourselves of that crown and summit of all the gifts and blessings of the Gospel, but open your hearts and your minds to expect and to believe in the actual abiding of the Divine nature in us. Mysticism? Yes! And I do not

---

122. Fanning, 199.

know what religion is worth if there is not mysticism in it, for the very heart of it seems to me to be the possible inter-penetration and union of man and God—not in the sense of obliterating the personalities, but in the deep, wholesome sense in which Christ Himself and all His apostles taught it, and in which every man who has had any profound experi-ence of the Christian life feels it to be true.[123]

For Maclaren, mysticism was highly practical. Here is one moving quote typical of many others:

Depend upon it, this nourishing of an inward life of fellow-ship with Jesus, so that we may say, "our lives are hid"—hid, after all vigorous manifestation and consistent action—"with Christ in God," will not weaken, but increase, the force with which we act on the things seen and temporal. There is an unwholesome kind of mysticism which withdraws men from the plain duties of everyday life; and there is a deep, sane, wholesome, and eminently Christian mysticism which en-ables men to come down with greater force, and to act with more decision, with more energy, with more effect, in all the common deeds of life.

This practical daily immersion in God's love impels us to go out and spread Christ's influence throughout this very real world of ours.[124]

Maclaren says of Bernard of Clairvaux, who rode on his horse rapt in contemplation yet was so practical and involved with this world that he exerted great political and religious influence through-out Europe:

The greatest mystics have been the hardest workers. Who was it that said, "I live, yet not I, but Christ liveth in me"? That

---

123. Alexander Maclaren, *The Epistles of John, Jude and the Book of Revelation* (New York: Hodder and Stoughton, 1910), 37.

124. Alexander Maclaren, *Epistle to the Hebrews Chapters VII to XIII* (London: Hodder and Stoughton, 1910), 318.

man had gone far, very far, towards a habitual consciousness of Christ's presence, and it was the same man that said, "That which cometh upon me daily is the care of all the churches." The greatest mystic of the Middle Ages, the saint that rode by the lake all day long, and was so absorbed in contemplation that he said at night, "Where is the lake?" was the man that held all the threads of European politics in his hands, and from his cell at Clairvaux guided popes....[125]

Maclaren always keeps his mysticism down to earth:

Mysticism is more than just sweet feeling; it must issue in obedience to Christ and service to fellow human being:

It is no use talking about communion with Jesus Christ, and abiding in Him, in possession of His love, and all those other properly mystical sides of Christian experience, unless you verify them for yourselves by the plain way of practice. Doing as Christ bids us, and doing that habitually and doing it gladly, then, and only then, are we in no danger of losing ourselves in the depths, or of forgetting that Christ's mission has for its last result the influencing of character and of conduct. "If ye keep My commandments, ye shall abide in My love, even as I have kept My Father's commandments, and abide in His love."[126]

Wholesome mysticism for Maclaren means spending time with God, giving space in the day to him. In short, it involves meditation. He writes, "There is only one way of getting God for yours, and that is by bringing Him into your life by frequent meditation upon His sweetness, and upon the truths that you know about Him."[127]

---

125. Maclaren, *Hebrews*, 318.

126. Alexander Maclaren, *The Gospel According to St. John Vol. 3* (New York: A.C. Armstrong and Son, 1908), 27.

127. Alexander Maclaren, *The Book of Psalms L to XLIX* (London: Hodder and Stoughton, 1909), 34.

Maclaren gives a succinct description of Christian meditation:

> Meditate, then, upon the things most surely believed, and
> ever meditate until the dry stick of the commonplace truth
> puts forth buds and blossoms like Aaron's rod. Every pebble
> that you kick with your foot, if thought about and treasured,
> contains the secret of the universe. The commonplaces of
> our faith are the food upon which our faith will most richly
> feed.[128]

Maclaren points out that the union Christ calls us to can liven the
totality of our being:

> He (Christ) can lay His hand upon your spirit's hand. He
> can flash light into your spirit's eye from His eye. He can
> put breath and eloquence into your spirit's lips from His
> lips, and His heart beating against yours can transfuse—if
> I may so say—into you His own lifeblood....[129] And He is
> in us as the sunlight in the else darkened chamber; we are
> in Him as the cold green log cast into the flaming furnace,
> glows through and through with ruddy and transforming
> heat. He is in us as the sap in the veins of the tree; we are in
> Him as the branches. As a branch cannot bear fruit of itself,
> except it abide in the vine, no more can ye except ye abide
> in me.[130]

Receptivity to God was the hallmark of contemplation for
Maclaren:

---

128. Alexander Maclaren, *A Year's Ministry* (New York: Funk and Wagnalls, 1905),
296.

129. Alexander Maclaren, "Expositions of the Holy Scriptures: Second Kings
from Chap. VIII, and Chronicles, Ezra, and Nehemiah, Esther, Job, Proverbs and
Ecclesiastes." See http://www.ccel.org/ccel/maclaren/2kings_eccl.ii.ii.v.html.

130. Alexander Maclaren, *Sermons Preached in Manchester* (New York: Macmillan
and Co, 1886), 72.

The more we trust, the more we can contain of His gift; and the more we can contain, the more we shall surely possess. As St. Bernard beautifully says, "He puts the oil of His mercy into the vase of our trust,"—and the larger the vase, the fuller the stream which He pours into it. As long as we bring vessels, the blessing runs, like the oil into the widow's cruse.[131]

Maclaren urges his readers to empty their hearts so:

that the mind may keep in steadfast contemplation of Jesus, and the heart may be bound to Him by cords of love that are not capable of being snapped, and scarcely of being stretched, and the will may in patience stand saying, "Speak, Lord! for Thy servant heareth"; and the whole tremulous nature may be rooted and built up in and on Him. Ah, brother! if we understand all that goes to the fulfilment of that one sweet and merciful injunction, "Abide in Me," we shall recognize that there is the field on which Christian effort is mainly to be occupied.[132]

Alexander Maclaren gives us one of the finest descriptions of contemplation ever written:

For a great many of us, the only notion that we have of prayer is asking God to give us something that we want. But there is a far higher region of communication than that, in which the soul seeks and finds, and sits and gazes, and aspiring possesses, and possessing aspires. Where there is no spoken petition for anything affecting outward life, there may be the prayer of contemplation such as the burning seraphs before the Throne do ever glow with. The prayer of silent submission, in which the will bows itself before God; the prayer of

---

131. Alexander Maclaren, *The Gospel of St. Matthew* (London: Hodder and Stoughton, 1892), 134.

132. Alexander Maclaren, *Christ's Musts and Other Sermons* (London: Alexander and Shepheard, 1894), 245.

quiet trust, in which we do not so much seek as cleave; the prayer of still fruition.[133]

Frederick Brotherton Meyer

Frederick Brotherton Meyer was another famous Baptist who extolled mysticism. He ministered in the latter part of the nineteenth and early part of the twentieth centuries. A close associate of the American evangelist Dwight Moody, Meyer authored over forty books, often with a devotional aim, which sold millions of copies. Following his death in 1929, the *New York Observer* called him "a man of international fame whose services are constantly sought by churches over the wide and increasing empire of Christendom." He pastored one of Britain's first mega churches, and his preaching drew many thousands.

A social activist especially oriented toward the welfare of elderly, the poor, the sick, he saw not just the need to help but also the need to change unmerciful structures in society into merciful ones. For this, Stephen Timms, in his recent biography of Meyer, says he was dubbed "*virtually a Christian socialist.*"[134]

He read widely in the mystics, especially Catherine of Siena, for whom he had a special affinity, and he believed that every vital Christian was a mystic. Like Maclaren, he looked to the Gospel of John for much of his mysticism. He wrote:

> Men say to me: "Is not this mysticism that you teach?"
> I answer: "Every mystic is not a Christian, but every Christian is bound to be a mystic, because mysticism is the indwelling of God." Religion amongst the Hindoos (sic) is the indwelling of God, but it disappoints them; they cannot reach it because they seek it by endeavoring for the absorp-

---

133. Alexander Maclaren, see http://www.ccel.org/ccel/maclaren/iicor_tim.txt.

134. Quoted in Wikipedia article, *Frederick Brotherton Meyer.*

tion of themselves, the loss of their individuality, in God. We as Christians seek also to know the indwelling of God, but it is not by the loss of our individuality, but by the reception of God's nature as the determining power working through the individuality which He has given to us. "Ye shall know that I am in the Father, and ye in me, and I in you."[135]

Times of contemplation were essential for the Christian life. Meyer tells us:

> But we must beware that we do not substitute in our own experience the active for the contemplative, the valley for the mountain-top. Neither can with safety be divorced from the other. The sheep must go in and out. The blood must come back to the heart to be recharged with oxygen before being impelled again to the extremities.[136]

He also says that we should live in our hearts, in restful contemplation of the fountain of love that is God, adding,

> There is no life to be compared with that of which the undivided heart is the center and spring. Why not seek it now? Turn to God in holy contemplation and ask Him to bring your whole inner realm under His government and to hold it as His forevermore....[137]

135. Frederick Brotherton Meyer, *A Castaway, and Other Addresses* (Chicago: The Bible Institute Colportage Association, 1897), 102.

136. Frederick Brotherton Meyer, *The Secret of Guidance.* See http://www.ccel.org/m/meyer/guidance/guidance.htm.

137. Frederick Brotherton Meyer, Lance Wubbels, ed., *Life of Abraham: The Obedience of Faith* (Lynnwood, WA: Emerald Books, 1996), 98.

An Ecumenical Vision

The journey into God's love that we call mysticism brings Christians of differing faith expressions together. The more we study the mystics of the past, Protestant, Catholic and Orthodox, the more we recognize ourselves as brothers and sisters dwelling in Christ. I have found it amazing how many Protestant mystics have looked to the works of Catholic mystics as sources of life. Perhaps Catholics can now learn from Protestant mystics.

As Bob Holman, who recently wrote a biography of F.B. Meyer, reminds us, Meyer borrowed from various sources and sought to bring Christians of diverse faith communities closer. "He (Meyer) expressed admiration for a Roman Catholic bishop whose devotional life serves as a 'rebuke' to his own. While at Christ Church, he helped form a Public Morals Council which drew together a range of denominations including Roman Catholic...."[138]

Alexander Maclaren, as usual, captures this ecumenical vision in beautiful poetic words:

> "to bear witness of that Light." It is the noblest function that a man can discharge. It is a function that is discharged by the very existence through the ages of a community which, generation after generation, subsists, and generation after generation manifests in varying degrees of brightness, and with various modifications of tint, the same light. There is the family character in all true Christians, with whatever diversities of idiosyncrasies, and national life or ecclesiastical distinctions. Whether it be Francis of Assisi or John Wesley, whether it be Thomas à Kempis or George Fox, the light is one that shines through these many-coloured panes of glass, and the living Church is the witness of a living Lord, not only before it, and behind it, and above it, but living in it.[139]

---

138. Bob Holman, *F.B. Meyer: If I Had a Hundred Lives* (Great Britain: Christian Focus Publications, Ltd., 2007), 109.

139. Alexander Maclaren, *Expositions of Holy Scripture: The Gospel according to St. John, IX to XIV* (New York: A.C. Armstrong and Sons, 1908), 8.

BIBLIOGRAPHY

Arndt, Johann. *True Christianity*. Mahwah, NJ: Paulist Press, 1979.

Augustine. *City of God*. Edinburgh, 1871.

———. *Augustine of Hippo, Selected Writings*. New York: Paulist Press, 1984.

Barclay, William. *The Letters to the Corinthians*. Louisville: Westminster John Knox Press, 2002.

Bernard of Clairvaux. *Selected Works*. New York: Paulist Press, 1987.

Bonaventure. *Bonaventure (Classics of Western Spirituality)*, trans. Ewert Cousins. Mahwah, NJ: Paulist Press, 1978.

Boorstin, Daniel J. *The Creators: A History of the Heroes of the Imagination*. New York: Random House, 1992.

Brother Ugolino. *The Little Flowers of St. Francis of Assisi*. CCEL.

Brueggemann, Walter. *The Psalmist's Cry: Scripts for Embracing Lament*. Kansas City: The House Studio, 2010.

Claghorn, George S., ed. "Edwards, Personal Narrative." *The Works of Jonathan Edwards, Vol. 16, Letters and Personal Writings*. New Haven and London: Yale University Press, 1998.

Climacus, John, trans. Colm Luibheid and Norman Russell. *John Climacus: The Ladder of Divine Ascent*. New York: Paulist Press, 1982.

Cornell, George W. "Spiritual Experiences Defy Scientific Beliefs," *Daily News Los Angeles*, January 10, 1987, Valley Section, 18.

Coulton, G.G. *Life in the Middle Ages, Volume III, Men and Manners*. New York: Macmillan, 1930.

Cousins, Ewert H., trans. *The Life of Saint Francis*. San Francisco: HarperOne, 2005.

Daniel, Walter with Maurice Powicke, ed. *The Life of Ailred of Rievaulx*. London: Nelson, 1963.

de Sales, Francis. *The Love of God, a Treatise*. Westminster, MD: Newman Press, 1962.

De Vinck, José. *The Works of Bonaventure: Cardinal, Seraphic Doctor, and Saint, Vol. 1: Mystical Opuscula*. Paterson, NJ: St. Anthony Guild Press, 1960.

Despres, Denise Louise. *Ghostly Sights: Visual Meditation in Late-Medieval Literature*. Norman, OK: Pilgrim Books, 1989.

Dulles, Avery, SJ. "The Symbolic Structure of Revelation," *Theological Studies* 41, March 1980.

Dupré, Louis. "The Christian Experience of Mystical Union." *Journal of Religion* 69, 1989.

Edwards, Jonathan. *The Works of Jonathan Edwards, Vol. 1*. London, 1834; repr. Peabody, MA: Hendrickson Publishers, 1998.

Erb, Peter C., ed. *Pietists: Selected Writings*. New York: Paulist Press, 1983.

Fanning, Steven. *Mystics of the Christian Tradition*. London: Routledge, 2001.

Fedotov, G.P. *A Treasury of Russian Spirituality*. New York: Sheed and Ward, 1948.

Fischer, Kathleen R. *The Inner Rainbow: The Imagination in Christian Life*. New York: Paulist Press, 1983.

Forman, Robert K.C., ed. *The Innate Capacity: Mysticism, Psychology, and Philosophy*. New York: Oxford University Press, 1998.

George, K.M. *The Silent Roots: Orthodox Perspectives on Christian Spirituality*. Geneva: World Council of Churches Publications, 1994.

Glynn, Joseph. *The Eternal Mystic: St. Teresa of Avila*. Burlington, VT: Vantage Press,1982.

Gui, Bernard. *The Life of St. Thomas: Biographical Documents*. Baltimore: Helicon Press, 1959.

Hambrick-Stowe, Charles E. *The Practice of Piety: Puritan Devotional Disciplines in Seventeenth-Century New England*. Chapel Hill, NC: University of North Carolina Press, 1982.

Heller, Dagmar. "Union with Christ: John Calvin and the Mysticism of St. Bernard." *Ecumenical Review*, July 1996.

Hoffman, Bengt R. "Lutheran Spirituality," in Robin Maas and Gabriel O'Donnell, eds., *Spiritual Traditions for the Contemporary Church*. Nashville: Abingdon Press, 1990.

Holman, Bob. *F.B. Meyer: If I Had a Hundred Lives*. Great Britain: Christian Focus Publications, Ltd., 2007.

Jones, Alan W. *Soul Making: The Desert Way of Spirituality*. San Francisco: HarperOne, 1989.

Jones, Cheslyn, Geoffrey Wainwright, and Edward Yarnold. *The Study of Spirituality*. New York: Oxford University Press, 1986.

Jones, Rufus. *Essential Writings*. Maryknoll, NY: Orbis Books, 2001.

———. *Some Exponents of Mystical Religion*. New York, Cincinnati: Abingdon Press, 1930.

———. *Studies in Mystical Religion*. London: Macmillan, 1909.

Kavanaugh, Kieran, ed. *John of the Cross: Selected Writings*. New York: Paulist Press, 1988.

Maclaren, Alexander. *Epistle to the Hebrews Chapters VII to XIII*. London: Hodder and Stoughton, 1910.

———. *Epistles General*. London: A.C. Armstrong, 1910.

———. *Exposition of the Scriptures: 1 John*. Rio, WI: Ages Software, 2001.

———. *Exposition of the Scriptures: Ephesians*. Rio, WI: Ages Software, 2001.

———. *Expositions of Holy Scripture: Romans and Corinthians*. Christian Classics Ethereal Library, www.ccel.org/ccel/maclaren/rom_cor. ii.i.html, accessed September 27, 2011.

———. *Expositions of Holy Scripture: St John Ch. I to XIV*. Christian Classics Ethereal Library, www.ccel.org/ccel/maclaren/john1.ii.xliii. html, accessed September 27, 2011.

———. *The Book of Psalms L to XLIX*. London: Hodder and Stoughton, 1909.

———. *Christ's Musts and Other Sermons*. London: Alexander and Shepheard, 1894.

————. *Expositions of Holy Scripture: The Gospel according to St. John, IX to XIV.* New York: A.C. Armstrong and Sons, 1908.

————. *Sermons Preached in Manchester.* New York: Macmillan and Co, 1886.

————. *The Epistles of John, Jude, and the Book of Revelation.* New York: Hodder and Stoughton, 1910.

————. *The Gospel According to St. John Vol. 3.* New York: A.C. Armstrong and Son, 1908.

————. *The Gospel of John Chapters IX–XIV.* New York: A.C. Armstrong and Son, 1908.

————. *The Gospel of St. Matthew.* London: Hodder and Stoughton, 1892.

————. *The Wearied Christ and Other Sermons.* New York: Hodder and Stoughton, 1893.

————. *The Second Book of Kings from Chap. VIII.* New York: A.C. Armstrong and Son, 1908.

McClymond, Michael J. *Encounters with God: An Approach to the Theology of Jonathan Edwards.* New York: Oxford University Press, 1998.

Meyer, F.B. *The Way Into the Holiest; Expositions of the Epistle to the Hebrews.* New York: F.H. Revell, 1893.

Meyer, Frederick. *Abraham or the Obedience of Faith.* New York: Fleming H. Revell Company, 1890.

Meyer, Frederick Brotherton. Lance Wubbels, ed. *Life of Abraham: The Obedience of Faith.* Lynnwood, WA: Emerald Books, 1996.

Meyer, Frederick Brotherton. *A Castaway, and Other Addresses.* Chicago: The Bible Institute Colportage Association, 1897.

————. *Saved and Kept: Counsels to Young Believers.* New York: Fleming H. Revell Company, 1897.

Moore, Archimandrite Lazarus. *An Extraordinary Peace: St. Seraphim, Flame of Sarov.* Port Townsend, WA: Anaphora Press, 2009.

Moreira, Isabel. *Dreams, Visions, and Spiritual Authority in Merovingian Gaul.* Ithaca: Cornell University Press, 2000.

Newberg, Andrew and Mark Robert Waldman. *How God Changes Your Brain*. New York: Ballantine Books, 2009.

Orosius, Paulus. *The Fathers of the Church: The Seven Books of History Against the Pagans*, trans. Roy J. Deferrari. Washington, DC: Catholic University of America Press, 2001.

Piehler, Paul. *The Visionary Landscape: A Study in Medieval Allegory*. Baltimore, MD: Edward Arnold, 1971.

Rakoczy, Susan. *Great Mystics and Social Justice: Walking on the Two Feet of Love*. New York: Paulist Press, 2006.

Schwarz, Reinhard. "Martin Luther (1483–1546)" *Grosse Mystiker. Leben und Wirken*. G. Ruhbach and J. Sudbrack, eds. Munich: C.H. Beck, 1984.

Stough, Furman C., and Urban Tigner Holmes. *Realities and Visions: The Church's Mission Today*. New York: Seabury Press, 1976.

Thomas of Celano. *St. Francis of Assisi: First and Second Life of St. Francis with Selections from the Treatise on the Miracles of Blessed Francis*. Placid Hermann, trans. Chicago: Franciscan Herald Press, 1963.

———. *The Lives of St. Francis of Assisi*. London: Methuen and Company, 1908.

Trape, Agostino. *St. Augustine: Man, Pastor, Mystic*. New York: Catholic Book Publishing Corporation, 1991.

Tugwell, Simon, ed. *Albert and Thomas: Selected Writings (Classics of Western Spirituality)*. New York: Paulist Press, 1988.

Underhill, Evelyn. *The Spiritual Life*. Harrisburg, PA: Morehouse Publishing, 1937.

———. *Mysticism*. Stilwell, KS: Digireads.com Book, 2005 edition.

Urs von Balthasar, Hans. *Explorations in Theology, Vol. I: The Word Made Flesh*, trans. A.V. Littledale, Alexander Dru. San Francisco: Ignatius Press, 1989.

van der Meer, Frederick, Brian Battershaw, and G.R. Lamb. *Augustine the Bishop: The Life and Work of a Father of the Church*. New York: Sheed and Ward, 1961.

Van Dyke, Paul. *Ignatius Loyola, The Founder of the Jesuits*. New York: Charles Scribner's Sons, 1926.

Vauchez, André. *La Sainteté en Occident aux derniers siècles du Moyen-Age. D'après les procès de canonisacion et les documents hagiographiques.* Rome: Ecole Française de Rome, 1981; Paris: Diffusion de Boccard, 1988.

Vaughan, Francis. "True and False Mystical Experiences: Some Distinguishing Characteristics," *ReVision* 12:1 (1989): 5.

Ward, Benedicta. *Miracles and the Medieval Mind: Theory, Record, and Event, 1000–1215 (The Middle Ages Series).* Philadelphia: University of Pennsylvania Press, 1987.

Whaling, Frank, ed. *John and Charles Wesley: Selected Prayers, Hymns, Journal Notes, Sermons, Letters and Treatises.* New York: Paulist Press, 1981.

Wilder, Amos Niven. *Early Christian Rhetoric: The Language of the Gospel.* New York: Harper and Row, 1964.

Wright, Wendy M., ed. *Francis de Sales: Essential Writings.* New York: The Crossroads Publishing Company, 1994.

Parish Missions
and Retreats

The primary author of this book, Deacon Eddie Ensley, along with Deacon Robert Herrmann, offers parish missions, retreats, and deacon programs throughout the country. A mission by the two deacons draws the whole parish together. It recharges the congregation. Everyone takes time for the truly important things like wonder, mystery, and prayer. People reconcile. Faith is awakened. Vocations are discovered. Families are healed. Lives are forever changed. The parish discovers afresh its ultimate calling and meaning.

To bring one of their missions or retreats to your parish or for an information packet on their missions for your parish, you can contact Deacon Ensley at **pmissions@charter.net** or visit their website at **www.parishmission.net**.

"The Mission proved to be a tremendous help for our families….Our attendance was better than ever. The guided meditations throughout were vivid and also uplifting. The parish mission was filled with solid content. The greatest compliment has been in the attendance."

FATHER JOHN T. EUKER,
ST. JOHN THE BAPTIST, PERRYOPOLIS, PENNSYLVANIA

More inspirational reading

Prayerful Pauses *Finding God's Presence in Daily Life*
AMY WELBORN

The gem of a book profoundly shines the light of faith into daily human experiences. Amy Welborn has the unique gift of being able to take the ordinary and see the extraordinary in it. Her reflections are practical, easy to read, and highly insightful.

128 pages • $12.95 • order 957828

Letters from Jesus *Experiencing the Depth of His Love*
DEACON EDDIE ENSLEY and FATHER ANGELO ARRANDO

Deacon Eddie Ensley and Father Arrando speak here through intimate letters from Jesus to help readers hear God speaking deep within them and thus to experience God, Jesus, and life itself as never before.

104 pages • $10.95 • order 958337

Beyond Pain *Job, Jesus, and Joy*
MAUREEN PRATT

This book challenges readers to follow the example of Job and, most of all, Jesus, in accepting pain and in believing there are many joys awaiting them, if they choose to reach out, look, hope, and live…beyond pain. It is for anyone who lives with deep, life-altering pain and who wants to have more joy, faith, and purpose. As Job did. As Jesus did.

168 pages • $14.95 • order 957866

Finding Our Sacred Center *A Journey to Inner Peace*
HENRI NOUWEN

Struggling to find peace of heart, Henri Nouwen went for a brief visit to Lourdes. Whether you have been there or not does not matter. This small journal is bound to touch your own restless and searching heart and help you find again your own sacred center. A wonderful and beautiful gift book!

64 pages • $9.95, hardcover • order 958474

TWENTY THIRD 23rd

1-800-321-0411 • www.23rdpublications.com